A HIKING GUIDE TO
ROCKY MOUNTAIN NATIONAL PARK

109 CLASSIC LUNCH SPOTS

Philip Gillett

Earthbound Sports, Inc.
Chapel Hill, NC

A HIKING GUIDE TO ROCKY MOUNTAIN NATIONAL PARK

109 CLASSIC LUNCH SPOTS

© 2002 Philip Gillett. All rights reserved. No part of this book may be copied or reproduced in any manner whatsoever without written permission of the publisher.

Printed in the United States of America

ISBN: 0-9643698-6-9

Published by:

Earthbound Sports, Inc.
PO Box 3312
Chapel Hill, NC 27515
www.earthboundsports.com

All photos from the Philip Gillett Collection

TO MY MOTHER AND FATHER

who brought me to Rocky Mountain National Park,
and to all those who made it possible to return
(especially the National Park Service, without whose tender care
none of us could call the Park home).

ACKNOWLEDGMENTS

To our son Bernard Gillett, who made the maps.

To Bill Webster, Bernard's publisher and also mine. Some of the suggested menus are his, as well as numerous details that he gently but persuasively suggested to improve the book.

To our children, who hiked with us when they were young, then encouraged us as we grew older.

Contents

INTRODUCTION 1
Getting to the Park 2
Town of Estes Park 2
The Park 3
Park Information 3
Backcountry Permits 3
Campgrounds 4
Getting to the Lunch Spots 4
Weather 5
What to Bring 6
What Not to Bring (or do) 6
Things You Need to Know to Avoid a Bad Time 6
Rock, Snow and Ice Climbing 7

BEAR LAKE TRAILHEAD (I) 9
1   BEAR LAKE NATURE TRAIL 9
2   NYMPH LAKE 11
3   DREAM LAKE 11
4   EMERALD LAKE 12
5   PARADISE 13
6   POOL OF JADE 14
7   LAKE HAIYAHA 14
8   THE HAIYAHA CIRCUIT 15

GLACIER GORGE TRAILHEAD 17
9   ALBERTA FALLS 17
10   THE LOCH 17
11   TIMBERLINE FALLS 18
12   LAKE OF GLASS 18
13   SKY POND 19
14   ANDREWS CREEK POOL 20
15   ANDREWS TARN 20
16   TAYLOR PEAK 21
17   THE GASH 21
18   MILLS LAKE 22
19   JEWEL LAKE 22
20   GLACIER CREEK POOL 23
21   RIBBON FALLS 23
22   BLACK LAKE 24
23   BLUE LAKE 25
24   GREEN LAKE 25
25   PAGODA MOUNTAIN 26
26   FROZEN LAKE 27
27   SPEARHEAD 27
28   McHENRYS PEAK 28
29   SHELF LAKE 29

30	SOLITUDE LAKE	29
31	THATCHTOP	30
32	ARROWHEAD	30

BEAR LAKE TRAILHEAD (II) 33

33	BIERSTADT LAKE	33
34	FLATTOP MOUNTAIN	33
35	HALLETT PEAK	35
36	OTIS PEAK	35
37	LAKE HELENE	35
38	PTARMIGAN TARN	36
39	GRACE FALLS	36
40	THE LITTLE MATTERHORN	37
41	TOURMALINE LAKE	37
42	ODESSA LAKE	38
43	FERN LAKE	38
44	SPRUCE LAKE	39
45	LOOMIS LAKE	39
46	FERN FALLS	40
47	THE POOL	40

LONGS PEAK TRAILHEAD 43

48	LONGS PEAK	43
49	EUGENIA MINE	45
50	CHASM LAKE	45
51	MOUNT MEEKER	45
52	MOUNT LADY WASHINGTON	46
53	STORM PEAK	46

BEAR LAKE ROAD TRAILHEADS 49

54	BOULDER BROOK MEADOW	49
55	SPRAGUE LAKE CIRCUIT	50
56	MILL CREEK BASIN	50
57	CUB LAKE	51

TRAIL RIDGE ROAD TRAILHEADS 53

58	THE UTE TRAIL	53
59	DEER MOUNTAIN	54
60	SUNDANCE MOUNTAIN	54

LAWN LAKE TRAILHEAD 55

61	YPSILON LAKE	55
62	SPECTACLE LAKES	55
63	LAWN LAKE	56
64	CRYSTAL LAKES	56
65	FAIRCHILD MOUNTAIN	65
66	HAGUES PEAK	65
67	MUMMY MOUNTAIN	65

FALL RIVER ROAD TRAILHEADS 66

68	ALLUVIAL FAN	66

69	ENDOVALLEY PICNIC AREA	66
70	CHASM FALLS	67
71	MOUNT CHAPIN	67
72	MOUNT CHIQUITA	68
73	YPSILON MOUNTAIN	68
74	THE WHALE	69
75	DESOLATION PEAKS	70

DEVILS GULCH ROAD TRAILHEADS 73

76	GEM LAKE	73
77	WEST CREEK FALLS	73
78	NORTH BOUNDARY TRAIL	74
79	BRIDAL VEIL FALLS	75
80	LOST LAKE	75
81	LAKE HUSTED	75
82	LAKE LOUISE	77
83	LAKE DUNRAVEN	77

COLORADO HIGHWAY 7 TRAILHEADS 79

84	LILY MOUNTAIN	79
85	LILY LAKE CIRCUIT	79
86	ESTES CONE	79
87	TWIN SISTERS	80

WILD BASIN TRAILS 82

88	SANDBEACH LAKE	82
89	CHIEFS HEAD PEAK	82
90	COPELAND FALLS	82
91	CALYPSO CASCADES	83
92	OUZEL FALLS	84
93	THUNDER LAKE	84
94	MERTENSIA FALLS	85
95	LION LAKES	85
96	SNOWBANK LAKE	86
97	MOUNT ALICE	86
98	BLUEBIRD LAKE	87
99	FINCH LAKE	87

WEST SIDE TRAILS 89

100	THE TONAHUTU TRAIL	89
101	TIMBER LAKE	91
102	SHIPLER CABINS	91
103	LULU CITY	93
104	OPPOSITION CREEK	93
105	ADAMS FALLS	93
106	POUDRE LAKE	94
107	MOUNT IDA	94
108	MOUNT RICHTHOFEN	96

109 THE GREEN DRAGON 96

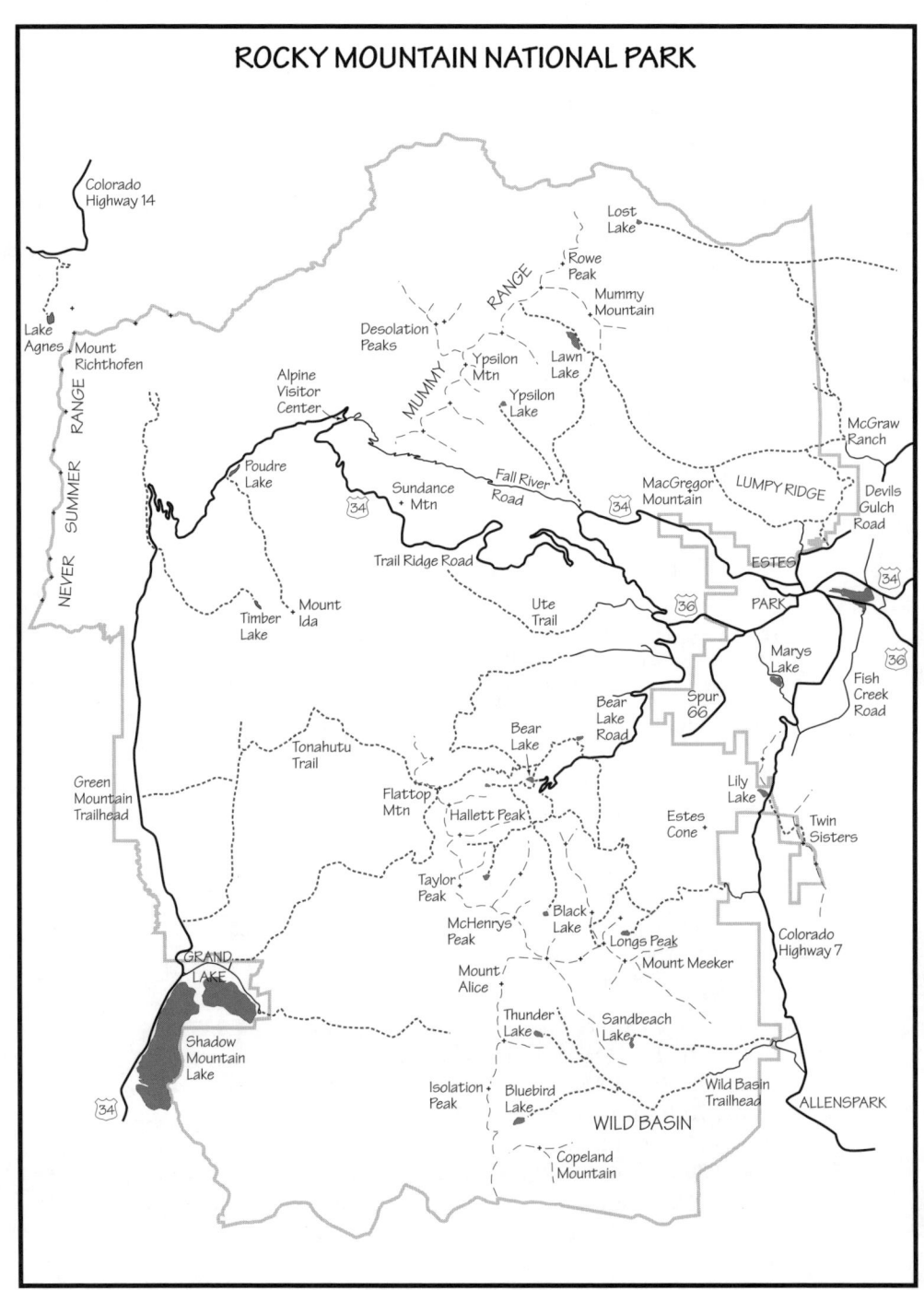

INTRODUCTION

This contribution to the lore of Rocky Mountain National Park is based on more than sixty-eight years of exploring the Park, where I soon realized that the whole point of a hike is lunch. This must be understood in the right spirit. The secular objective of the hike is of course important, whether it be the top of Longs Peak or the point where all concerned have agreed to give up. The religious objective, however, should not be overlooked, the holy and wholesome reason why people walk when they could stay in bed, as opposed to the lame excuses given when asked why they hike at all. How many times do we hear *exercise* as a motive! If that were the reason for hiking, we could walk at the Mall and have lunch at McDonald's. Others will offer a mantra about Nature, or Nature's God, but in those cases there are less strenuous approaches, like a drive up Trail Ridge Road, or church, respectively, and lunch can be left out altogether.

No, I'm afraid that anthropologists will discover, when their research is completed, that human-type persons leave civilization for a hike into the wild because lunch tastes better there. I will never forget a car trek (not even hiking) that our family took in 1968. We would stop at some lovely spot to prepare lunch, which seemed more often than not to consist of grilled cheese-bologna-sliced apple sandwiches. They were superb. After returning home, I asked my wife to make one for lunch. It was not superb. Draw your own conclusion.

The title of this collection may remind you of that wonderful book *Fifty Classic Climbs in North America,* which inspired our children as they grew up spending summers in Estes Park. Most of them are technical climbers, and have done such classics as El Capitan in Yosemite, Devils Tower in Wyoming, and the Diamond and Petit Grepon in Rocky Mountain National Park. One of them (Bernard) is the author of a well-known guidebook on technical routes in the Park. Another (Maria) is Chief of Interpretation at Mt. Rainier National Park, while still another (John) has been a search and rescue ranger at Longs Peak and Mt. Rainier, and on ski patrol at Copper Mountain in Colorado. A fourth (Mary) was also a Longs Peak search and rescue ranger, while our youngest (Robert) has helped out on rescues in the Park. Our daughter Joan is no exception to all this, but as the mother of six, she is now introducing them to the old haunts with advice from their grandparents. Our oldest daughters Patricia and Anne are not into climbing, but they like to hike.

The best part of our advice, as parents of eight and grandparents of twenty-two (at last count) is to pack a good lunch. You don't have to get to the top of what you're climbing, nor to the end of the trail you're on, but you do have to find a suitable spot for lunch. It is to that proposition that we here dedicate this book, so that grilled cheese-bologna-sliced apple sandwiches shall not perish from the earth.

Some readers may find the selection of lunch spots eccentric (fifteen in Glacier Gorge, for example, and only nine west of the Continental Divide). The reason for that is simple. I wanted to include only places we have been. As summer residents of Estes Park (now retired there), we naturally did most of our hiking on the east side of the mountains. Besides, we have a special affection for Glacier Gorge.

Directions for finding these places are of course included, but the book is not so much a comprehensive hiking guide as it is a description of good spots to have lunch. These range from the ridiculous (Bear Lake) to the sublime (the top of McHenrys Peak), with many wonderful resting places in between. Along the way some politically incorrect pontification may be encountered, defended by appropriate dogma. Be not afraid—it is harmless unless (God forbid) you are humorless about these matters.

LECTOR and **AUCTOR** ("Reader" and "Author") are characters in Hilaire Belloc's classic travelogue *The Path to Rome.* To paraphrase C.S. Lewis (writing of another author in *That Hideous Strength):* Mr. Belloc is so rich in invention that he can well afford to lend, and I admire his invention so much that I feel no shame in borrowing.

THE NUTS & BOLTS

GETTING TO THE PARK

Rocky Mountain National Park may be entered from the east by driving through Estes Park on US 36 (Beaver Meadows Entrance) or US 34 (Fall River Entrance). Both entrances are just outside the town limits. Other entrances on the east side are described in the body of the book. On the west side US 34 enters the Park just north of the town of Grand Lake, continuing over the mountains to Estes Park.

TOWN OF ESTES PARK

In the summer Estes Park is a tourist town that provides the usual amenities. There are many churches, some medical clinics, a hospital, dentists, grocery stores, a health food market, numerous restaurants, fast food joints, and some coffee and bakery shops. Motels and rental cabins are abundant, though often without vacancies, so reservations are recommended. Nightlife is low-key, with a few bars, a microbrewery, and a couple of multiple-theater complexes. There are also two golf courses. The finest entertainment, however, is on the trail, where the mountains beckon under indigo skies. Contact the Estes Park Chamber Resort Association for more information (500 Big Thompson Avenue, Estes Park, CO 80517, phone 970-586-4431, www.estesparkresort.com).

THE PARK

More than 260,000 acres of scenic wilderness provide visitors with high-country experience second to none, whether by car or on foot. The Park may be traversed by car on Trail Ridge Road, the highest continuous paved road in the country, crossing the Continental Divide near timberline (about 11,000 feet). There is a visitor center at Fall River Pass (just below the high point at 12,083 feet), where the air is thin enough to suggest caution in those with a heart condition or breathing difficulties.

More than 100 peaks rise above the tundra of the treeless alpine zone, including one "fourteener" (Longs Peak) and numerous "thirteeners". Several small glaciers and countless snowfields feed such a profusion of streams and lakes as to defy listing. The main drainages on the east side of the Divide are the Big Thompson, St. Vrain, and Cache la Poudre Rivers, while the headwaters of the Colorado River rise on the west.

Several hundred miles of hiking trails (including some for wheelchairs) make the wilderness accessible to all, though it may take a few minutes away from the trailheads to experience "wilderness." At least half a million hikers use the trails every year, but it is easy to avoid them if you are so inclined. On the other hand, one of the politically incorrect affirmations of this book is that we are all "children of the universe" and have a right to be here. Meeting other human beings on the trail is not such a contradiction of wilderness as some would have us believe.

PARK INFORMATION

Brochures and maps and general information can be had at several visitor centers and entrances. Headquarters of the Park are a short distance before the Beaver Meadows entrance on US 36 (phone 970-586-1206 for visitor information). The National Park Service website is www.nps.gov.

BACKCOUNTRY PERMITS

Permits ($15 in 2002) are required for overnight stays in the backcountry; consult the Backcountry Office near the Visitor Center on US 36 (970-586-1242).

CAMPGROUNDS

There are several campgrounds in the Park, but they are usually full. Reservations placed well in advance are advisable; call the Park public information office (970-586-1206) or MIStix (800-365-2267). Park regulations allow only seven nights at these campgrounds (three at Longs Peak).

For a longer stay, commercial campgrounds are recommended. Those listed in the phone book are as follows:

  Blue Arrow RV Park & Campground, 1665 Hwy 66, 970-586-5342

  Estes Park Campground, 3420 Tunnel Rd, 970-586-4188

  Estes Park KOA Campground, 2051 Big Thompson Ave, 970-586-2888

  Manor RV Park, 815 Riverside Dr, 970-586-3251

  Mary's Lake Campground, 2120 Marys Lake Rd, 970-586-4411

  National Park Resort, 3501 Fall River Rd, 970-586-4563

  Paradise RV & Travel Park, 1836 Hwy 66, 970-586-5513

  Spruce Lake RV Park, 1050 Marys Lake Rd, 970-586-2889

  Yogi Bear's Jellystone Park of Estes, 5495 Hwy 36, 970-586-4230

GETTING TO THE LUNCH SPOTS

Descriptions of the lunch spots are numbered, in sections that correspond roughly to their location in the Park. Basic information is supplied in each case:

Distance – one-way (unless otherwise noted), rounded to the nearest half-mile.

Altitude – the highest elevation in the hike, rounded to the nearest hundred feet (except that altitudes of peaks are given more precisely).

Elevation Gain – the difference between trailhead altitude and altitude at the highest point, rounded to the nearest hundred feet.

Difficulty – rated from "trivial" to "very hard". These ratings vary with the season and condition of the hiker, and in any case are subjective. For what it's worth, they may be defined as follows. (All bets are off if the route is icy or snow-covered, although snowshoes can reduce the difficulty.)

  Trivial – a mostly flat, short walk on a well-maintained trail (sometimes called a "freeway").

  Easy – less than 1,000 feet of elevation gain, at most two or three miles one-way, on a freeway.

Moderate – less than 2,000 feet elevation gain, no longer than five miles one-way, on a clear trail (perhaps partly "unimproved").

Hard – due to distance, elevation gain, route-finding, scrambling, or a combination of these.

Very hard – a major climb, requiring good conditioning, an early start, knowledge of the terrain, good judgment, and willingness to turn back when conditions (bad weather or inability to cope) call for it.

WEATHER

While it is fun to hike in the Park year-round (snowshoeing is becoming popular), winter weather can be brutal in the high country. Most visitors are here in summer, when daytime highs are usually comfortable (but can range from the thirties to the eighties depending on altitude and weather). Mornings are cool (often below freezing higher up) and usually clear. Afternoon storms are common, normally followed by clear, cool evenings.

Lightning is the most dangerous weather-related hazard in the Park. It is important to be aware of incoming storms, and to be prepared to take shelter when there is electricity in the air. (If your hair stands on end, it may already be too late!) It is best to be away from high places (peaks, ridges, exposed rocks, and solitary trees) before noon.

The most dangerous weather hazard (after lightning) is the intense sunlight. Even in Estes Park, at 7,500 feet, brief encounters with direct sunshine can be harmful, and the risk increases with altitude. Effective sunscreen lotions are essential.

THINGS THAT CAN GET YOU

Every place in the world presents certain hazards. Rocky Mountain National Park has its own additional dangers:

Lightning (mentioned above) and **severe storms**, which can blow you away and may dump snow or damaging hail on the route (dangerously slippery if it's steep).

Snowfields (sometimes ice looking like snow) require caution – there have been fatal slides ending on rocks at the base of the field.

High or fast water has claimed several victims (especially children), due to slippery rocks, incautious wading, or attempted crossings.

Drinking from streams, which can carry disease (see below).

Animals – squirrels sometimes carry bubonic plague, mountain lions and bears are obviously dangerous (though rarely seen), even deer, elk, and bighorn sheep are not safe to approach.

Ticks (at lower elevations early in the season) can carry tick fever or Rocky Mountain spotted fever – it is prudent to check for them after hiking.

WHAT TO BRING

Things to bring along vary with the severity of the hike. Even a short walk to a nearby lake is enhanced by a tasty lunch carried in a fanny pack or backpack (and lunch spots are what this book is about). Try not to let marmots, bluejays, and other enterprising creatures make off with your food. Some of them will chew right through a backpack.

Stream and lake water looks pure but is not; carry an ample supply of tap water, or bring along some means of purifying mountain water. It is not a happy experience to come down with what we used to call Rocky Mountain glitch (more precisely, giardiasis, carried by wildlife droppings into the streams).

On longer and higher excursions the authorities recommend sturdy hiking boots and comfortable socks, poncho, warm jacket, gloves, hat, sunglasses, first-aid kit, map, compass, pocketknife, flashlight, matches, and a copy of *War and Peace*. Long-sleeved shirts and slacks avoid exposure to the sun and to woodticks, but this advice is honored more in the breach than the observance. We like to carry hiking poles, being aging grandparents.

WHAT NOT TO BRING (OR DO)

Park regulations prohibit firearms, pets on the trails, removal of anything but trash, disturbance of wildlife, picking wildflowers, littering, and a partridge in a pear tree. Registration for hikes and climbs is not required, but it is folly not to let somebody know where you're headed. Something as simple as a sprained ankle off-trail can be a matter of concern, particularly if you are so imprudent as to hike alone.

THINGS YOU NEED TO KNOW TO AVOID A BAD TIME

In case of emergency, contact a ranger (970-586-1399 or dial 911). The Park has a well-trained rescue service available year-round, but it takes time to mobilize. The best way to avoid calling one is to stay within the limits of your competence, and to turn back before they are approached. One of my favorite lines is Maria's in *The Sound of Music*, in response to the Mother Superior's worry about her safety in the high country: *O Mother, I could never be lost up there!* But that attitude requires intimate knowledge of the Park. Failing that, it is not bad advice to carry a topographic map of the region you intend to enter.

ROCK, SNOW AND ICE CLIMBING

While many hikes described in this book require scrambling, none are technical climbs. If you are inclined to hang out on (or attached to) ropes and carabiners and the like, you might want to acquire a popular guide to climbing routes in the Park (and nearby), *Rocky Mountain National Park: The Climber's Guide,* 2nd Edition, by our son, Bernard Gillett. Whenever we encounter climbers on our hikes, I ask if they know him. Often the answer is yes, but when it is no, I ask if they use a climber's guide. The light usually dawns at that point and they respond, "Oh, of course, we carry Bernard's book with us everywhere." When I say, "Well, he's our son," a happy conversation follows. Apparently his guide is the best thing since nylon rope.

RESPONSIBILITY, LIABILITY, LAWYERS, AND SUCH

Anybody hiking in the Park can come to grief one way or another. The author and publisher of this book note that it is intended as a *general* guide to the hikes described. While the information should be most useful in finding your way to a superb lunch spot, it may be less detailed than some would like. The distance and altitude given for each hike are approximate, and the rating of difficulty is subjective. Users of the book are responsible for their own safety, and for the results of their own decisions.

NOTE FROM THE PUBLISHER

It's rare for an author to invite the Publisher (that busybody who always wants to change things) to participate in the book. As an ex-Rocky Mountain National Park ranger, avid hiker, fanatical climber, and long-suffering publisher of other peoples' work, I appreciate the opportunity to contribute a few lunch menus gathered from friends around the country.

   AUCTOR: He will be longer-suffering if we identify his menus.

8 A HIKING GUIDE TO RMNP

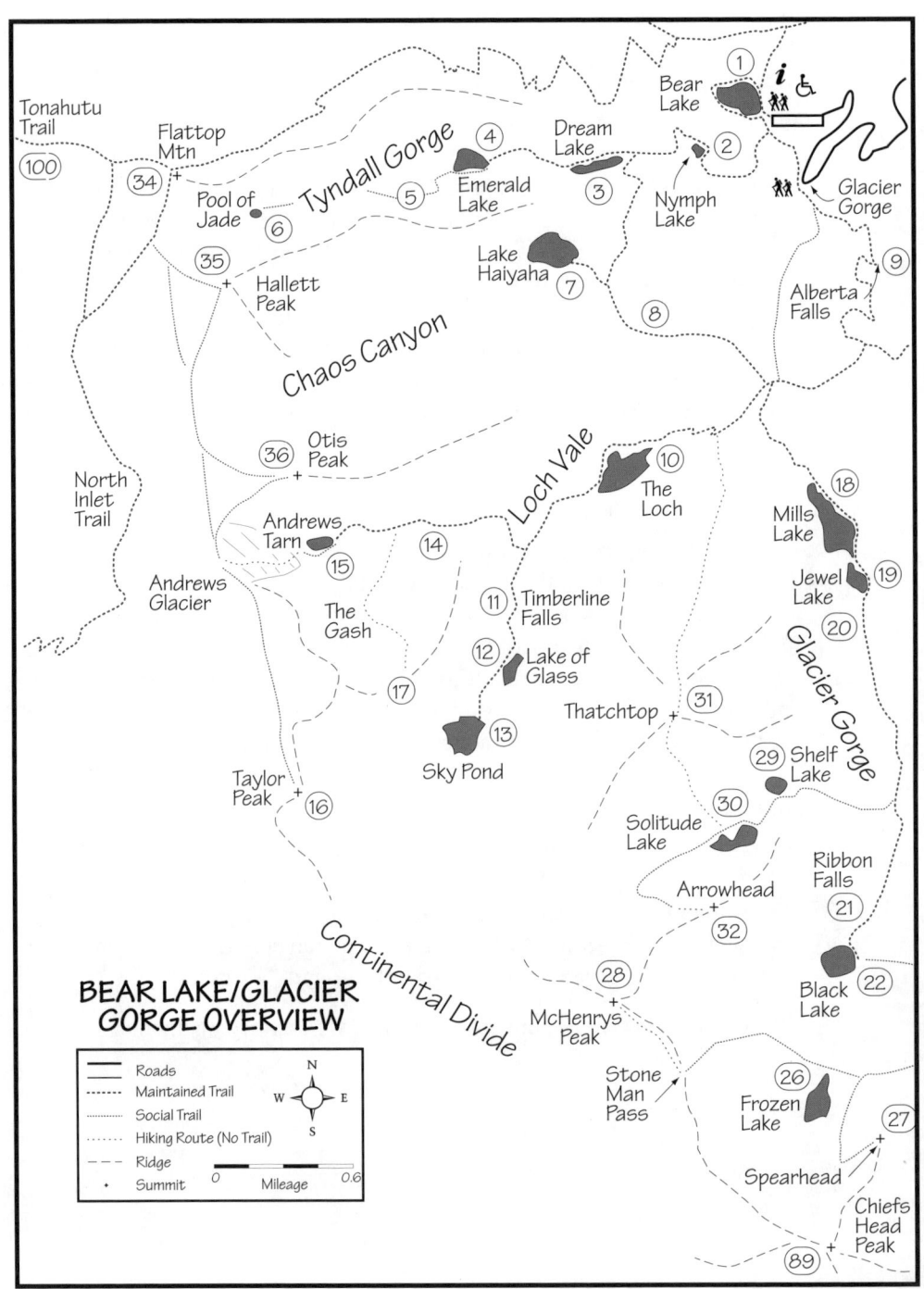

BEAR LAKE TRAILHEAD (I)

The following eight lunch spots are located south and west of Bear Lake. Hikes 33-47 north and west of Bear Lake can be found starting on page 33.

1 BEAR LAKE NATURE TRAIL

Distance	Altitude	Elevation Gain	Difficulty
0.25 miles round trip	9,500 ft	0	trivial

Maps: 8, 10, 16, 32, 34, 48, 88. Take US 36 from Estes Park to the Beaver Meadows entrance to "Rocky Mtn Natl Park" (as some of the signs say— I used to entertain our children by trying to pronounce it as spelled). Turn left almost immediately onto the Bear Lake Road, which winds up through beautiful scenery to (what else?) Bear Lake. The parking lot fills early on summer days, but the Park Service has come to the rescue with shuttle buses that will take you back to your school days. Actually they will take you up and down the Bear Lake Road, starting at a parking lot across from Glacier Basin. Once you are at Bear Lake, explore the (mostly level) trail that circles it, which is very pretty, and accessible to just about everybody. There are benches here and there, ideal for lunch if they are unoccupied.

> PUBLISHER: This isn't the place for lunch. Too many people may want to share it and there are too many distractions. Maybe a snack — since you're at Bear Lake, pull out a package of gummy bears.
>
> AUCTOR: Look here. Whose book is this?

The thing is, thousands visit Bear Lake every year. Why, you may ask, do we include such a place as a lunch spot? Because it's lovely, that's why. Perhaps we should clear our minds of the "politically correct" belief that people spoil wilderness—or does the definition of wilderness exclude nature's most interesting creatures? Thomas Aquinas says somewhere that human beings exist for their own sake— everything else receives its meaning from their perception. (Modern quantum theory seems to bear this out.) If the statement seems doubtful, ask yourself what you would rather hang over your fireplace: a picture of a pristine forest, or another picture of the same forest with a trail winding through it? Places not seen by anybody are in some sense meaningless (except of course that every part of creation is "meant" by its Creator). As the famous Marlboro ads suggest (never mind the motives of their sponsor), a wild place is often improved by a cabin at its heart, with smoke rising from the chimney and a cowboy on his way home.

10   A HIKING GUIDE TO RMNP

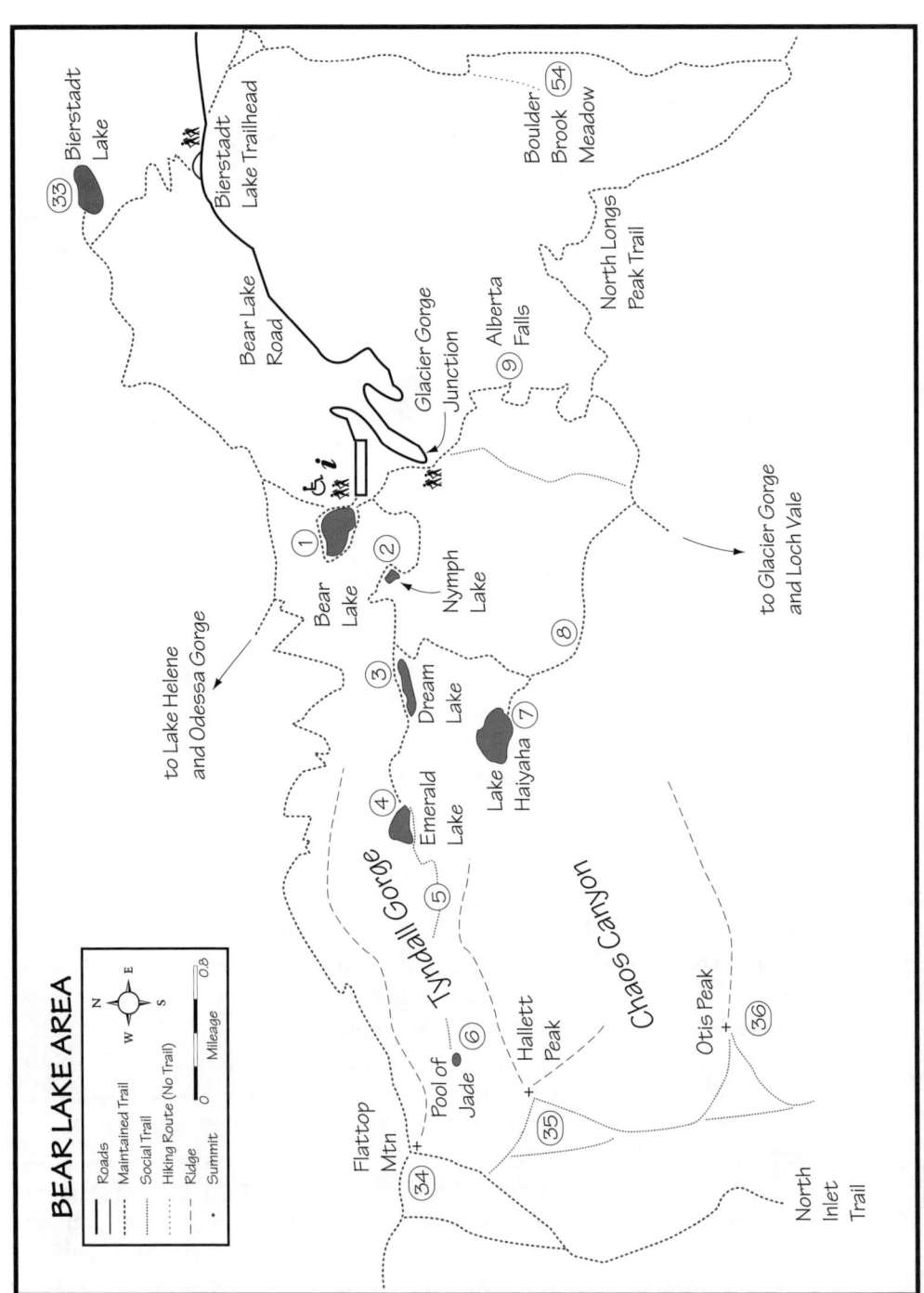

LECTOR: I don't want a picture of a forest above my fireplace.

AUCTOR: Are you going to complain before we get past the first lunch spot?

LECTOR: I want a portrait of a spotted owl.

AUCTOR: I like spotted owls. I like them so well I want to hike a trail to see them.

2 NYMPH LAKE

Distance	Altitude	Elevation Gain	Difficulty
0.5 miles	9,700 ft	200 ft	easy

Maps: 8, 10, 16, 32, 34. This short hike (up the Dream Lake trail from Bear Lake) is probably the most popular in the Park, with beautiful views of Longs Peak along the way. Although easy, it is enough uphill to induce rapid breathing if you are not yet acclimated. Despite the number of fellow hikers passing by, it is not hard to find a quiet place for lunch. If you like to encounter people while eating, sit on one of the benches provided and contemplate Hallett Peak. Don't overlook the water lilies.

3 DREAM LAKE

Distance	Altitude	Elevation Gain	Difficulty
1 mile	9,900 ft	400 ft	easy

Maps: 8, 10, 32, 34. Maybe Bear Lake and Nymph Lake are too crowded at lunchtime. Rise up from your bench and continue up the trail another half-mile to Dream Lake. (It may be harder if the section above Nymph Lake is still covered with snow.) There are perhaps ten fewer people here. Many are taking pictures of Hallett Peak and Flattop Mountain, looming over the lake to the west. A Union Pacific calendar of some years back claimed that this was the most photographed spot in America. The mind boggles at the question of how they knew that—did somebody count the pictures?

LECTOR: Have you heard of statistical sampling?

AUCTOR: I taught mathematics for 40 years.

LECTOR: Then you must know we don't need to count all the pictures.

If Dream Lake isn't the most photographed spot in America, it ought to be. That reminds me of the revisionist historian who doubted that General

Pershing (arriving in France with the American Expeditionary Force in World War I) said, "Lafayette, we are here." Obviously if he didn't, he should have.

Among the slabs overlooking Dream Lake you can find a classic lunch spot. Or are you going on to Emerald Lake? The trail follows the north shore of Dream Lake, past families of tourists and ducks. In less than a mile it ends at an even more photogenic spot, the rocky shore of one of the greenest lakes you'll ever see. Hallett and Flattop fill the sky above the other side—the place is justly famous. Harden your candy bar in the cold water, submerge your beverage, and settle down for lunch. Look up to the mountains, from whence cometh our salvation.

LECTOR: Will there be much of that sort of thing in the book?

AUCTOR: I'll try not to be a problem, but some things are irresistible.

LECTOR: What do you propose to do about these digressions?

AUCTOR: They are included to make the book more entertaining.

LECTOR: I bought it to learn about lunch spots.

4 EMERALD LAKE

Distance	Altitude	Elevation Gain	Difficulty
2 miles	10,100 ft	600 ft	moderate

Maps: 8, 10, 32, 34, 88. The attractions of Emerald Lake are described under Classic Lunch Spot No. 3, page 11. But it is too beautiful not to have a listing of its own. For one thing the trail beyond Dream Lake is no longer a freeway. Perhaps this is a good place to suggest a menu. Grilled cheese is out of the question, but bologna sandwiches (you may not believe this) are wonderful at 10,000 feet, particularly if you have hiked for a while to get there. They are nicely washed down with the juice of an orange (which survives a pack better than most fruit). Potato sticks provide some salt to replace what you may have lost if the hike was warm. Remember to retrieve the candy bar you hardened in the lake, and the beverage that is cold by now. All things considered, isn't this as good as an expensive restaurant?

We will add here that the next classic lunch spot is reached from this one. If you are willing to scramble to find it, pack up your lunch and start boulder-hopping around the south shore. When you reach the inlet on the west side, prepare for an adventure.

5   PARADISE

Distance	Altitude	Elevation Gain	Difficulty
2.5 miles	10,800 ft	1,300 ft	hard

Maps: 8, 10, 32, 34. Many years ago I was returning from a hike to the Pool of Jade (No. 6) near the base of Tyndall Glacier (a steep and dangerous snow field between Hallett and Flattop). On the way back down to Emerald Lake I came across a tiny glen nestled between huge boulders below the famous Hallett buttresses, with Tyndall Creek running in through a dark opening under the rocks and out again through another passage, down a dizzying waterfall into the deep bowl holding Emerald Lake. The glen was covered with grass the color of Irish meadows and there were flowers everywhere. It was shut off from the world by the overhanging rocks, its quiet interrupted only by the music of the stream. A holy place—I dubbed it Paradise (not to be confused with heaven, which is of a different order of reality).

To enjoy this place, you must either die and ask your guardian angel to take you there (before attending to business), or discover it yourself. There is no simple way up the inlet. You can detour around to the left, up a slope of talus and scree (sometimes covered with slippery snow), or you can work your way into a bay closer to the waterfall and do some climbing along a smaller stream. This sometimes involves getting past a steep slab of hard snow that has pulled away from the rocks to form a crevasse. The last hike I took with my mother (she was 72 at the time) was here. She negotiated the crevasse (and the whole hike) nimbly, but developed leg cramps after returning home. My father decreed that it was her last hike (with me, anyway) and she obeyed. She took me up Longs Peak when I was 12—in her eighties she offered to do the same for our children.

> LECTOR: You have already mentioned your children. Are we going to hear much about your mother?
>
> AUCTOR: What have you got against mothers?
>
> LECTOR: Nothing, if they help with lunch.

One way or another, with care, you will arrive near the top of the waterfall that blocks direct ascent of the inlet. Then you still have to find the narrow stretch of grass along the stream that leads up to the entrance of Paradise. You may be faintly aware of a creature with a flaming sword, though nowadays he is harder to see. G.K. Chesterton says somewhere that Paradise was not so much lost as it was disguised. If we could open our eyes to see, it would be all around us.

The last line of *Lost Horizon* (spoiled by the moviemakers, who insist on answering the question) is "Do you think he will ever find it?" In *The Lord of the Rings* the elf-queen sings to Frodo "Maybe even thou shalt find it." The theme is universal—we remember Paradise. This place I am trying to help you reach is not the real thing, but it will do. If you find it, spread out your things on the grass, put that candy bar and drink in the stream, lie back and look as deep as you can into the blue, review your life, and determine to reform. After a suitable time at lunch, climb down cautiously to the lake and hike out silently to your car.

LECTOR: We might get along better if you would stop trying to influence my life.

AUCTOR: It is mine I want to influence. If enough people buy this book, I will be able to afford a new pair of hiking boots.

6   POOL OF JADE

Distance	Altitude	Elevation Gain	Difficulty
3 miles	11,400 ft	1,900 ft	hard

Maps: 8, 10, 32. Scramble up the talus and scree slope above Emerald Lake, making for the top of the waterfall as described in No. 5. You may not notice the little glen we call Paradise, but if the Pool of Jade is your goal, keep going past the Hallett buttresses until you have nearly reached Tyndall Glacier at the end of the gorge. Its tarn is (as the name suggests) pale green. Do not venture onto the glacier, which is dangerously steep and usually icy—an uncontrolled slide onto the rocks below could be fatal and would spoil your meal. Enjoy lunch at the tarn.

7   LAKE HAIYAHA

Distance	Altitude	Elevation Gain	Difficulty
2 miles	10,200 ft	700 ft	easy

Maps: 8, 10, 32. Back at the east end of Dream Lake (No. 3, page 11) an easy trail heads off to the left, soon switchbacking up through the trees above the lake. (If this section is snow-covered, it can be dangerous.) It ends after a mile that is down as well as up, at a lake protected by large boulders (apparently the source of the Indian name "Haiyaha"). It is good to have lunch here, though you may be joined by many others.

If you are feeling ambitious, you can climb Otis Peak (No. 36, page 35) from here, returning by way of Andrews Glacier (see No. 16, page 21). The gorge between Otis (on the left) and Hallett (on the right) is called Chaos Canyon. It deserves the name—we don't recommend it as a route to anywhere.

8 THE HAIYAHA CIRCUIT

Distance	Altitude	Elevation Gain	Difficulty
6-8 miles round trip	10,200 ft	700 ft	moderate

Maps: 8, 10, 16, 32. On your return from Lake Haiyaha (No. 7) look for a trail that branches off to the southeast about a quarter-mile back. (You passed the sign on the way to the lake.) This path goes mostly downhill for a mile to the junction of the Glacier Gorge and Loch Vale trails. Along the way there are numerous little streams (and at least one pond) where you can lose the civilized world and have lunch. Then you can hike out past Alberta Falls (No. 9) to the Glacier Gorge parking lot. Since your car is probably at Bear Lake, you will need to walk up the half-mile trail connecting the two parking places, completing a circle we call the "Haiyaha Circuit." Five lakes (Bear, Nymph, Dream, Emerald, Haiyaha) and a waterfall (Alberta) may be included with modest effort. If your definition of "modest" differs from ours, you can omit the trip from Dream Lake to Emerald Lake (and back), and not go all the way to Lake Haiyaha, and still enjoy a lovely circle. This one is haunted by elves out of Tolkien.

LECTOR: Somebody told me we can also skip Alberta Falls, by taking a short cut.

AUCTOR: Not so loud. But see No. 10.

16 A HIKING GUIDE TO RMNP

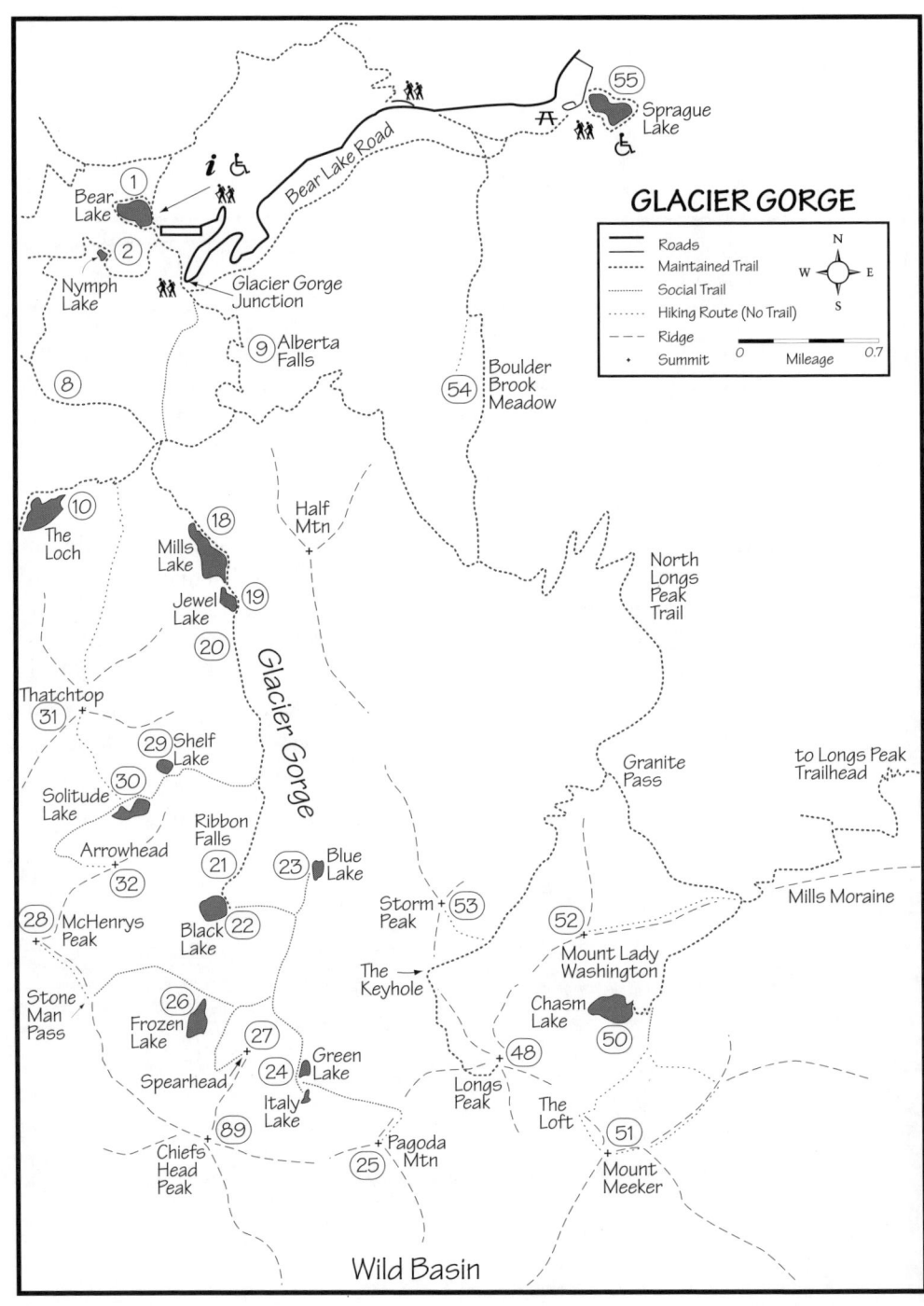

GLACIER GORGE TRAILHEAD

9 ALBERTA FALLS

Distance	Altitude	Elevation Gain	Difficulty
0.5 miles	9,400 ft	200 ft	easy

Maps: 8, 10, 16, 32. The trail to this popular spot starts at the Glacier Gorge parking lot (on Bear Lake Road a short distance below the large lot). Unless you get there early (before 7:30!), the lot will be filled—use the shuttle bus system (see No. 1, page 9) or park at Bear Lake and hike down the half-mile trail connecting the two lots. The waterfall (more a torrent down a twisting channel) is impressive from the trail below, and also from the rocks at the top (which is easily accessible). It is a nice place to have lunch if you don't mind the traffic.

10 THE LOCH

Distance	Altitude	Elevation Gain	Difficulty
2.5 miles	10,200 ft	900 ft	moderate

Maps: 8, 16. Starting at the Glacier Gorge parking lot on Bear Lake Road, follow the trail to Alberta Falls (No. 9) and beyond, to the well-marked junction of Glacier Gorge and Loch Vale (about two miles from the trailhead). There is a three-way split here: the trail from Lake Haiyaha (No. 8) comes in from the right, the left branch leads to Glacier Gorge, and the middle trail heads uphill for about half a mile to The Loch (as lovely a spot as you'll find anywhere in the Park). Some people call it Loch Vale, but that's the name of the valley of The Loch. Visitors are plentiful, but as with every popular spot, it is no trick to imitate Greta Garbo if you want to be alone. Enjoy lunch.

It is politically incorrect to mention short cuts in a book about the Park (because they often cause erosion, braided trails, and other abominations). The one we are about to recommend, however, does none of these things—in fact it cuts down on the freeway traffic that goes past Alberta Falls. Starting at the Glacier Gorge parking lot, check off three bridges as you pretend to be making for the falls (four if you count one that is more a shore-up of the trail than a bridge). When the trail turns left off the last bridge (only a quarter-mile from the trailhead), leave it for the wooded slope directly ahead, following a path up through the trees for a short distance and then turning right at a jumble of boulders that obscure the way. (Make a note of these boulders for the return trip, to avoid bushwhacking beyond them instead of turning down.) The trail is clear from this point on, and it cuts off considerable distance from the main route.

About half a mile up the short cut, the trail disappears for a few yards on a shelf with cliffs above and a drop-off into the valley below. There are slab-covered passages (virtually caves) along the base of the cliffs, ideal for small children to walk through (provided you first halloo away any inhabitants). In another half-mile the short cut rejoins the main trail just below the junction of Glacier Gorge and Loch Vale described above. There is some artfully distributed debris at this point, presumably designed to discourage use of the short cut. We have never understood why.

11 TIMBERLINE FALLS

Distance	Altitude	Elevation Gain	Difficulty
4 miles	10,400 ft	1,200 ft	moderate

Map: 8. The Loch (No. 10) is only one of the attractions of Loch Vale. Follow the trail around the north side of the lake and continue up Icy Brook (the stream that drains Loch Vale) to the bridge over Andrews Creek, which flows down from Andrews Glacier (see No. 15, page 20) to join Icy Brook. This is already a good lunch spot, though you will want to move off the bridge to avoid traffic. But you can do better. Taking the left-hand trail up Loch Vale from the bridge, you will pass the great Cathedral Wall on your right, where technical climbers may sometimes be seen. Soon the path steepens, as you work up the slope below Timberline Falls—a splendid place to have lunch. It is especially beautiful in early summer, when there is still snow to be sculptured by the stream.

12 LAKE OF GLASS

Distance	Altitude	Elevation Gain	Difficulty
4+ miles	10,800 ft	1,600 ft	hard

Map: 8. You may not be ready to call it a day at Timberline Falls (No. 11)—spectacular rest stops are ahead. Ratchet yourself up the steep rocks to the right of the falls until you reach the Lake of Glass immediately above. It is a rare day when the breeze is calm enough for the lake to look like glass, but lunch anywhere along the shore is a delight. You are above timberline now, and the surrounding peaks seem cut out from an impossible sky (assuming the blue has not yet been clouded over by the usual afternoon weather).

It is almost irresistible to follow a faint path along the west side of the lake, toward a small buttress that seems to bar further progress. A way opens as if by magic, and suddenly you are up the cliff, and the trail to Sky Pond is there before you.

13 SKY POND

Distance	Altitude	Elevation Gain	Difficulty
4.5 miles	10,900 ft	1,700 ft	hard

Maps: 8, 88. A half-mile hike up the tundra above the Lake of Glass (No. 12) brings you to Sky Pond, at the end of Loch Vale. Thatchtop on the left, Powell Peak and Taylor Glacier ahead, and Taylor Peak on the right, wall in this wonderful spot, with several spectacular spires towering above the west side of the lake. Be sure to walk around the lake far enough to see the famous Petit Grepon head-on (or blade-on). You will wonder, as we do, how anybody climbs it. Since several of our children do, we have to believe it. But we will not list its top as a classic lunch spot.

> PUBLISHER: Come on now, there are no better lunch spots in the Park. A classic, moderately difficult technical climb lands you on a summit the size of a dining room table, a superb spot for lunch. Just be off (numerous rappels) before the inevitable storm rolls in, or you may be electrified.
>
> LECTOR: Can you explain why people climb these things, in 25 words or less?
>
> AUCTOR: I like the attitude George Mallory took toward Everest.
>
> LECTOR: Because it is there.
>
> AUCTOR: Precisely.
>
> LECTOR: He fell off.
>
> AUCTOR: Oh, you pragmatists! The world has grown gray with your breath.
>
> LECTOR: You needn't mangle Swinburne.

14 ANDREWS CREEK POOL

Distance	Altitude	Elevation Gain	Difficulty
4 miles	10,800 ft	1,600 ft	moderate

Map: 8. Back at the bridge over Andrews Creek (see No. 11, page 18), turn right to go up the trail along the creek, continuing past a spur that goes to a campground, until you cross a rocky section at tree-line. A sign warns of a restoration area, which should not be entered. Backtrack a few yards downhill and cross the stream, then follow it uphill to a grassy spot next to a limpid pool behind the restoration area. No finer place to have lunch can be imagined—the menu might be chosen to match it, say French Chardonnay (cooled in the stream), smoked salmon, cream cheese, sourdough bread…

    LECTOR: My menu is somewhat more appropriate.

    AUCTOR: Don't you think this place is beautiful?

    LECTOR: It's lovely, especially the limpid pool, as you call it.

    AUCTOR: What would you call it?

    LECTOR: Pellucid.

15 ANDREWS TARN

Distance	Altitude	Elevation Gain	Difficulty
4.5 miles	11,400 ft	2,200 ft	hard

Map: 8. This little gem lies on a lofty shelf at the base of Andrews Glacier. From the Andrews Creek pool (No. 14) follow the trail that has been relocated from the creek to the rocky slope on its right. The reason for this is restoration of a trampled valley. Moreover, the buttress below Andrews Tarn is hard to manage head-on, particularly if there is still steep snow to be traversed on its flanks. The first time I encountered it was with a ranger friend, going downhill after a descent of Andrews Glacier. He had just taught me how to use an ice axe. I slipped on the snow, and would have come to grief except for the axe.

The climb up to the tarn is still a workout, but easier than it used to be due to the well-marked trail. When you get there, look up to the glacier, which comes to the water's edge, and look down at the flowers. Have lunch.

    LECTOR: I'm glad to see you have something good to say about rangers.

    AUCTOR: Three of our children have been rangers. If it weren't for the Park Service, I would not have been able to contradict the old saw "You can't go home again."

16 TAYLOR PEAK

Distance	Altitude	Elevation Gain	Difficulty
6 miles	13,153 ft	3,900 ft	hard

Maps: 8, 88. From Andrews Tarn (No. 15) climb up Andrews Glacier, which is steep enough to cause concern, but not so steep as to be dangerous (unless unusual conditions have made it icy). We prefer to take ice axes along, but most people don't. Avoid any crevasses that appear—old photographs show some awesome ones, but in recent years they haven't amounted to much. At the top of the glacier turn left (south) and slog up the long tundra slope to the summit of Taylor Peak. The view is magnificent, particularly of Longs Peak, looming above the two valleys (Loch Vale and Glacier Gorge) that separate it from your present perch. Look straight down to Sky Pond (No. 13, page 19). As a youngster with little sense, I once tried to descend directly to Sky Pond from Taylor Peak. It almost worked. But I came to a shelf that was non-negotiable, and had to climb back out defeated. Such things should not be tried without a partner and a rope.

The way back from Taylor Peak, down the tundra and glacier past the tarn, and out by way of Andrews Creek and the Loch Vale trail, is wonderful. But you may be ready for a second (or third) lunch at the end—it's a twelve-mile round trip.

LECTOR: What I will be ready for at the end is not printable.

AUCTOR: The emergency room?

17 THE GASH

Distance	Altitude	Elevation Gain	Difficulty
4.5 miles	12,000 ft	2,800	hard

Map: 8. From the Andrews Creek pool (No. 14), observe the south wall of the valley. Sharkstooth (a subsidiary spire of Taylor Peak) rises to the southwest, with other teeth along the wall and behind it. The way up to this wall (a little west of south) is called The Gash. It gets steeper as you climb (stay to the right of the narrowing rockfall)—dangerous if the rocks are slippery with snow. But the dizzying perch on the other side (which can be descended a short way with care) is one of the most spectacular eyries in the Park. Petit Grepon (see No. 13, page 19) grins across the chasm, together with other towers almost as forbidding. If you have a strong stomach, find a safe place to sit down and have lunch.

18 MILLS LAKE

Distance	Altitude	Elevation Gain	Difficulty
2.5 miles	9,900 ft	700 ft	moderate

Maps: 8, 16, 78. Starting at the Glacier Gorge parking lot on Bear Lake Road, proceed as in No. 10, page 17 (The Loch), following the trail past Alberta Falls or using the short cut. At the junction of Glacier Gorge and Loch Vale, take the left-hand trail to the bridge over Icy Brook, which drains Loch Vale. We like to think of Glacier Gorge as starting on the other side of this bridge—on our first trip each year I kneel and kiss the ground. I would not want to claim that John Paul II learned this gesture from me, but I was doing it before he did.

Mills Lake is half a mile beyond this point, in a spectacular valley bounded on the east by Longs Peak, on the south by Pagoda, Chiefs Head, and McHenrys Peak, and on the west by Thatchtop. It is a memorable place to have lunch. There are also wonderful choices ahead.

> LECTOR: Do you have any pictures of yourself kissing the ground?
>
> AUCTOR: None that I know of.
>
> LECTOR: It's a pity. You could have amused your readers.
>
> AUCTOR: I'm trying to do that with these conversations.
>
> LECTOR: That reminds me—have you read *The Path to Rome* by Hilaire Belloc?
>
> AUCTOR: I know what you're going to say.
>
> LECTOR: Have you no shame?
>
> AUCTOR: See the Introduction.

19 JEWEL LAKE

Distance	Altitude	Elevation Gain	Difficulty
3 miles	9,900 ft	700+ ft	moderate

Maps: 8, 16, 78. Follow the trail along the east side of Mills Lake (No. 18) to its south end—Jewel Lake is not far beyond. The lake is well-named—it sparkles like a jewel (especially in the late afternoon, with its emerald shore glistening in the sun on the far side). Lunch here is a treat. Some little distance farther there used to be a corduroy bridge across the wet part of a meadow. We would count the logs (often getting as many answers as there were counters). Since I did the same thing with my parents, nostalgia was thick around the place. When the bridge was replaced, I removed one of the long metal spikes that had held it together and brought it home to lay on our computer hutch. Thus does the old decorate the new.

LECTOR: Nostalgia isn't what it used to be.

AUCTOR: I wish I'd said that.

20 GLACIER CREEK POOL

Distance	Altitude	Elevation Gain	Difficulty
3+ miles	10,000 ft	800 ft	moderate

Maps: 8, 16, 78. When you first come to the meadow mentioned in No. 19, turn aside from the trail (to the right), cross the meadow (being careful to tread only on dry ground), and find the stretch of Glacier Creek that is so placid as to be like flowing glass. A few feet downstream from this idyllic spot (itself worthy of lunch), there is a large boulder causing the stream to narrow into a small waterfall. It is easy to jump across here, but I managed to fall in once, due to a slip on the take-off. I was recently retired at the time, eager to prove to my hiking companions that age need not altogether erode athletic prowess. They were vastly entertained as I surfaced, having lost my glasses, my dignity, and the point. The point is that behind the boulder (no need to cross the stream) there is a shaded ledge facing the waterfall. Dangle your legs over the edge and have lunch.

LECTOR: I would I had been there.

AUCTOR: It would have much amaz'd you.

LECTOR: Very like, very like.

AUCTOR: Can we stop quoting Hamlet?

LECTOR: We can stop these conversations altogether if you like.

AUCTOR: No, they help us get from one lunch spot to the next.

21 RIBBON FALLS

Distance	Altitude	Elevation Gain	Difficulty
4.5 miles	10,600 ft	1,300 ft	moderate

Maps: 8, 42, 78. When I was a child I spake as a child—we didn't know the right name of this wonderful cascade, but called it Silver Falls. It is not far below Black Lake in Glacier Gorge (No. 22), but is easily missed. You have to leave the southbound trail to the lake and contour a hundred yards or so west to Glacier Creek, through open woods. It doesn't much matter where you do this. If you do it too soon, you may have to cross the stream and hike up through the trees until you reach the bottom of the falls, but it's fun to negotiate the slabs to the top. It is unlikely that you will cut out too late, since that will put you on the last slope below Black Lake. Actually you can see the falls from the trail, but only briefly.

In any case, there is a large rock at the top of the falls, ideal for lunch. You won't believe how beautiful the place is until you get there. Then you may agree that it is not just one of a hundred or so, but belongs in the Top Ten. The only reason we don't advise staying there all afternoon is that Black Lake itself is in the Top Ten. And there are several spots above Black Lake in the Top Ten. If you get the idea that Glacier Gorge uses up more than its share of the Top Ten, you're right. There are few places that are as lovely. Of course several thousand other people share this opinion. On any given day some of this group may be encountered along the trail (dwindling as you go higher). They are all nice folks, and you are not a misanthrope, are you? You are? Then get thee to Wrangell-St. Elias National Park in Alaska, where there is no wailing or gnashing of teeth (due to a severe shortage of creatures that wail or gnash their teeth).

As for me, I rather like to contemplate all the tourists enjoying the Park. Many have a tendency to confine their visit to Trail Ridge Road and Bear Lake, and even there it is only five minutes work to find a private spot. I am one of those heretics who is undisturbed by the novel idea that every person is a child of the universe and has a right to be here. And I have experienced the Park for sixty-eight years without noticing any significant deterioration of its beauty due to tourists. We were all tourists once.

LECTOR: You said you would not preach this sort of thing.

AUCTOR: No, I said I would try not to be a problem.

LECTOR: The road to hell is paved with good intentions.

AUCTOR: Nonsense. It may be a slippery slope, but only those who intend evil slide down it.

LECTOR: I don't want to talk about it any more.

22 BLACK LAKE

Distance	Altitude	Elevation Gain	Difficulty
5 miles	10,600+ ft	1,400 ft	hard

Maps: 8, 16, 42, 78, 88. After Ribbon Falls (No. 21) it is not far to Black Lake, and the scenery is more spectacular with every step. The pinnacle northwest of the lake is Arrowhead (12,387 ft), connected by an awesome ridge to McHenrys Peak (13,327 ft), a little south of west. Directly south, at the end of Glacier Gorge, is Chiefs Head Peak (13,579 ft), with Spearhead (12,575 ft) looming up in front. Pagoda Mountain (13,497 ft) rises to the southeast, connected to Longs Peak (14,255 ft) by the Keyboard of the Winds. Not all of this panorama is visible from the lake (which is nestled under cliffs that obscure part of the view behind). But you can pick out the various high points as you hike along the trail.

Our daughter Joan used to claim that the meadow at the east end of the lake is the most beautiful spot on earth. By the time she finished her graduate work in English at the University of Wisconsin-Madison, she had learned the meaning of hyperbole. But she wasn't that far wrong. Of course Black Lake is the destination of many others who feel the same way—be prepared for company. It is also beautiful in winter, and easier to reach (because you can snowshoe up Glacier Creek). Like Lancelot in *Camelot,* we find it hard to leave in any season. But it is the gateway to remote lunch spots in the great amphitheater above.

LECTOR: Your daughter now eschews hyperbole?

AUCTOR: More than most.

LECTOR: Then there is hope.

AUCTOR: For what?

LECTOR: That hereditary disease may be conquered.

23 BLUE LAKE

Distance	Altitude	Elevation Gain	Difficulty
5.5 miles	11,100 ft	1,900 ft	hard

Maps: 8, 42, 78. To reach the amphitheater above Black Lake (No. 22), head east toward Longs Peak, up the trail that follows the inlet above timberline. Turn left when the stream turns right, climbing up to the shelf that holds Blue Lake. The view is impressive.

24 GREEN LAKE

Distance	Altitude	Elevation Gain	Difficulty
6 miles	11,500 ft	2,300 ft	hard

Maps: 8, 42, 81. The trail up the Black Lake inlet (see No. 23) turns right to head for Green Lake. But it pretty much disappears among the flat slabs and krummholz that are found everywhere around the amphitheater. Stay on the right side of the stream (at a respectful distance, to avoid rock-hopping). From Black Lake it is about a mile to Green Lake. Find a place to sit near the shore, and enjoy lunch. If you prefer, go up another quarter-mile to Italy Lake, smaller but closer to the immense walls (Pagoda and Chiefs Head) at the south end of the gorge. At either lake you are in a bowl that defies description.

LECTOR: Then you won't describe it?

AUCTOR: Do you like oxymorons?

LECTOR: Never met one.

25 PAGODA MOUNTAIN

Distance	Altitude	Elevation Gain	Difficulty
6.5 miles	13,497 ft	4,300 ft	hard

Maps: 8, 42, 81. Green Lake (No. 24) is the place to start climbing Pagoda. Except for some slabs that are best avoided, the ascent is reasonable, but it seems a long time before you are up the couloir that leads (east) to the low point of the ridge between Pagoda and Longs Peak. The part of this ridge that runs over to Longs Peak is called the Keyboard of the Winds. Once when we were descending Pagoda I decided to climb the nearest spire of the Keyboard. Upon reaching the top, I realized that a storm was brewing, confirmed by the unsettling fact that my hair began to stand on end. Calling down to our daughter Maria (waiting with a camera), I said "Take the picture, quick!" She did, I got off the top, and all was well. But electricity near high points is not to be trifled with.

From the low point of the ridge it is a short but steep climb up the summit slope of Pagoda. The view of Longs Peak is stunning. On the day we climbed with Maria we found a two-liter bottle of Pepsi among the rocks at the top. There was an obsolete note welcoming friends of the climbers who left it there. We decided they were not coming, and that the Pepsi would freeze if we didn't take it. It was a good addition to our lunch.

LECTOR: There is a confusion of moral theology here.

AUCTOR: If the Pepsi had frozen, think of the confusion among marmots.

LECTOR: Then the end justifies the means?

AUCTOR: Look here, this is a book about lunch spots.

LECTOR: That's what I thought once.

26 FROZEN LAKE

Distance	Altitude	Elevation Gain	Difficulty
6 miles	11,600 ft	2,400 ft	hard

Maps: 8, 16. Before reaching Green Lake (No. 24, page 25), turn right (west) to contour around the base of Spearhead (a spire we used to call The Pinnacle, connected to Chiefs Head by a ridge). Walking along the slabs, you will come to Frozen Lake (or to a lip overlooking it, depending on where you turned right). Well into summer the lake is partly frozen, which bodes well for the temperature of the beverage you will surely submerge in preparation for lunch.

> LECTOR: I can call spirits from the vasty deep.
>
> AUCTOR: Why, so can I, or so can any man; but will they come when you do call for them?
>
> LECTOR: Not if they were pilfered from Pagoda.
>
> AUCTOR: Have you seen Henry IV?
>
> LECTOR: No, is he missing?

27 SPEARHEAD

Distance	Altitude	Elevation Gain	Difficulty
6+ miles	12,575 ft	3,300 ft	hard

Maps: 8, 16. From Frozen Lake (No. 26) climb up the northwest flank of Spearhead, which is slow going because of the scree. Head for the ridge connecting Spearhead to Chiefs Head, then turn left (north) to approach the top. The summit is too small for more than one person to sit on, and is dangerous to climb without a rope. The first time I was there, I had our two youngest (Mary and Robert) along—getting us in condition to climb Longs Peak. I didn't realize how intimidating the top is, but just scrambled up without thinking. Coming back down to where I had parked the kids, I perceived my folly, and vowed not to be so foolish again.

The next year the whole family repeated this climb, but near the top I decreed that nobody would go further. John, however, had stowed a rope in his pack, which he begged permission to use. I relented and went with him to the top. Some years later he became a search and rescue ranger on Longs Peak.

> LECTOR: Are you suggesting a cause and effect?
>
> AUCTOR: Only that the sins of the fathers are visited on the sons.

Be content with the view from just below the top of Spearhead, which will turn your stomach if you are not used to sheer drop-offs. Assuming all systems recover, have lunch. Do not attempt to go down a different route—all but the scree slope are technical.

28 McHENRYS PEAK

Distance	Altitude	Elevation Gain	Difficulty
7 miles	13,327 ft	4,100 ft	very hard

Maps: 8, 16, 88. To climb McHenrys, contour past Frozen Lake (No. 26) until you are under the low point of the ridge connecting McHenrys and Chiefs Head. This point is called Stone Man Pass (for reasons that will be apparent when you look at the rock formation to its left). It is hard to reach on the best of days, dangerous when the snow is icy on the way up. Turn right at the pass and find the best way to the top of McHenrys.

Once I was with three of our children on a route that was not the best (we were too far to the left). A ranger happened to be climbing not far away. He called over to say, "You're on a technical route!" Great. There was nothing for it but to continue upward, which we did without mishap. But young Bernard (who later became a well-known technical climber) actually shed tears on a ledge he and I occupied on the way up. It reminded me of an earlier climb with our daughter Joan, who shares with me a love of Tolkien's *Lord of the Rings*. We had an anxious time on McHenrys, too, leading me to quote Frodo at the Council of Elrond: "I will take the Ring, though I do not know the way." Joan understood.

All things considered, we recommend the top of McHenrys as a classic lunch spot, but with reservations. You should be a good route-finder, or go with somebody who knows the way. Suggested menu: cold breast of chicken, Bing cherries, salted mixed nuts, candy bar, and lemonade. Stay on the top long enough to appreciate it.

LECTOR: Why do you include these places in a book about lunch spots?

AUCTOR: You could have stopped at Black Lake.

LECTOR: I wanted to see what it looks like up here.

AUCTOR: Isn't it splendid?

LECTOR: If you don't mind the storm that is brewing.

29 SHELF LAKE

Distance	Altitude	Elevation Gain	Difficulty
4+ miles	11,200 ft	2,000 ft	hard

Maps: 8, 16. A little less than four miles up the Black Lake trail (No. 18-20, pages 22-23), with Arrowhead looming ahead on the right, you will come out of the woods to the edge of a lovely meadow. Before starting the rocky section along its left side, turn right (west) toward a crossing of Glacier Creek below the stream that comes down from Shelf Lake. Look for a large boulder that makes the crossing easy—otherwise you may have to wade. There is a poor imitation of a trail going steeply uphill to Shelf Lake, on the north side of the outlet, but it's hard to find and easy to lose. We often do lose it, bushwhacking our way to the lake (being careful not to pull on loose rocks or unreliable branches). It is a hard quarter-mile.

Shelf Lake is not far above timberline, at the edge of a hanging valley overlooking Glacier Gorge, with a fine view of the west face of Longs Peak. Thatchtop rises above it on the northwest, Powell Peak looms at the end of the gorge. It is a first-rate spot for lunch. But leave time for a cautious descent back to the Black Lake trail. There are many places where it is easy to come to grief.

30 SOLITUDE LAKE

Distance	Altitude	Elevation Gain	Difficulty
4.5 miles	11,400 ft	2,200 ft	hard

Maps: 8, 16. Shelf Lake (No. 29) need not be your final destination. Going up its inlet over some moderate slabs, you will come in short order to Solitude Lake. In early summer there may be stretches of snow along the way, with beautiful blue crevasses. In any case, lunch among the rocks along the shore is a joy. Remember that any liquids you have brought will taste better after cooling in the lake. We would recommend Kentucky sour mash mixed with mountain water, but it may not kill the organisms that cause the trots (or worse), and besides, you want to be serious on the descent. A non-alcoholic beverage at the temperature of the lake is as good as it gets.

LECTOR: What's this about Kentucky sour mash?

AUCTOR: See No. 95, page 85 (Lion Lakes).

31 THATCHTOP

Distance	Altitude	Elevation Gain	Difficulty
5 miles	12,668 ft	3,400 ft	hard

Maps: 8, 16. From Solitude Lake (No. 30) turn right (northwest) to slog up Thatchtop for spectacular views. You can go down the same way, but it is less work (remember the "trail" below Shelf Lake) to traverse the peak and descend the other side, into Loch Vale. The trick is to find the S-shaped gully that takes you safely down to Icy Brook. This gully is visible from the Loch Vale trail, but that is no help when you're above it. We recommend Thatchtop with someone who has done it before.

32 ARROWHEAD

Distance	Altitude	Elevation Gain	Difficulty
5.5 miles	12,387 ft	3,100 ft	very hard

Map: 16. Hiking up the gorge above Solitude Lake (No. 30), you will have the Arrowhead ridge on your left. It looks hard to climb, but presently (near a small pond about a quarter-mile beyond the lake) the steepness relents enough to allow picking your way between slabs to the top of the ridge. One summer our youngest daughter Mary and I were doing this, when she reached the crest and looked over the edge, several hundred sheer feet down. Muttering *Holy Shit* to herself, she sat down to await my labored ascent. When I peered down the same void, I said *Holy Shit* out loud. Mary started to laugh—upon my inquiring what was so funny, she explained, and we had a high-altitude fit.

You can follow the Holy Shit Ridge (more or less northeast) to the summit of Arrowhead. The way is not hard, but it is a scramble. The top is barely large enough to qualify as a lunch spot, but it is certainly classic. The view in all directions is superb. To descend, remember to follow the ridge back to where you came up from the Solitude Lake gorge—turning down too soon will bring you to precipices you won't want to attempt without a rope.

> LECTOR: I am not edified by the language in this book.
>
> AUCTOR: Insufficiently elevated?
>
> LECTOR: Oh, we're high enough.
>
> AUCTOR: I'm sorry to have offended you.
>
> LECTOR: You could have said *Holy Toledo*.
>
> AUCTOR: And offend the heretics?

That Pasta / Mushroom / Pine Nut thing
Jim Horst, Wisconsin

1/2 cup of soaked, thinly sliced black mushrooms
1/4 cup of pine nuts
1/3 cup of olive oil
1 tablespoon of crushed garlic
salt
pepper
8 to 12 oz (packaged weight) of your favorite pasta. Tricolor rotini or orzo work well, but we prefer fresh tortellini or mini ravioli.

Step 1. Prepare pasta per instructions on the packaging and set aside to drain but do not chill.
Step 2. While Pasta is draining heat the olive oil in a large non-stick frying pan.
Step 3. Add the garlic and sauté for 20 seconds while stirring to distribute throughout the pan.
Step 4. Add the pine nuts and the mushrooms and stir.
Step 5. Sauté on medium high heat until the pine nuts just begin to brown.
Step 6. Add the pasta and gently mix to coat the pasta evenly with olive oil.
Step 7. Add pepper and salt to taste*.
Step 8. (Optional) Turn up heat and brown the pasta slightly for added texture / flavor. This works best with flat pasta like mini ravioli.
Step 9. Cool and store in Tupperware, glad or similar reusable containers.

Refrigerate for storage over night and allow to reach room temperature in your pack before serving. This is also great served hot as a side dish for any meat entrée.
*If you plan on eating on the trail, make sure to salt properly so you don't need to carry salt and don't forget your fork.

32 *A HIKING GUIDE TO RMNP*

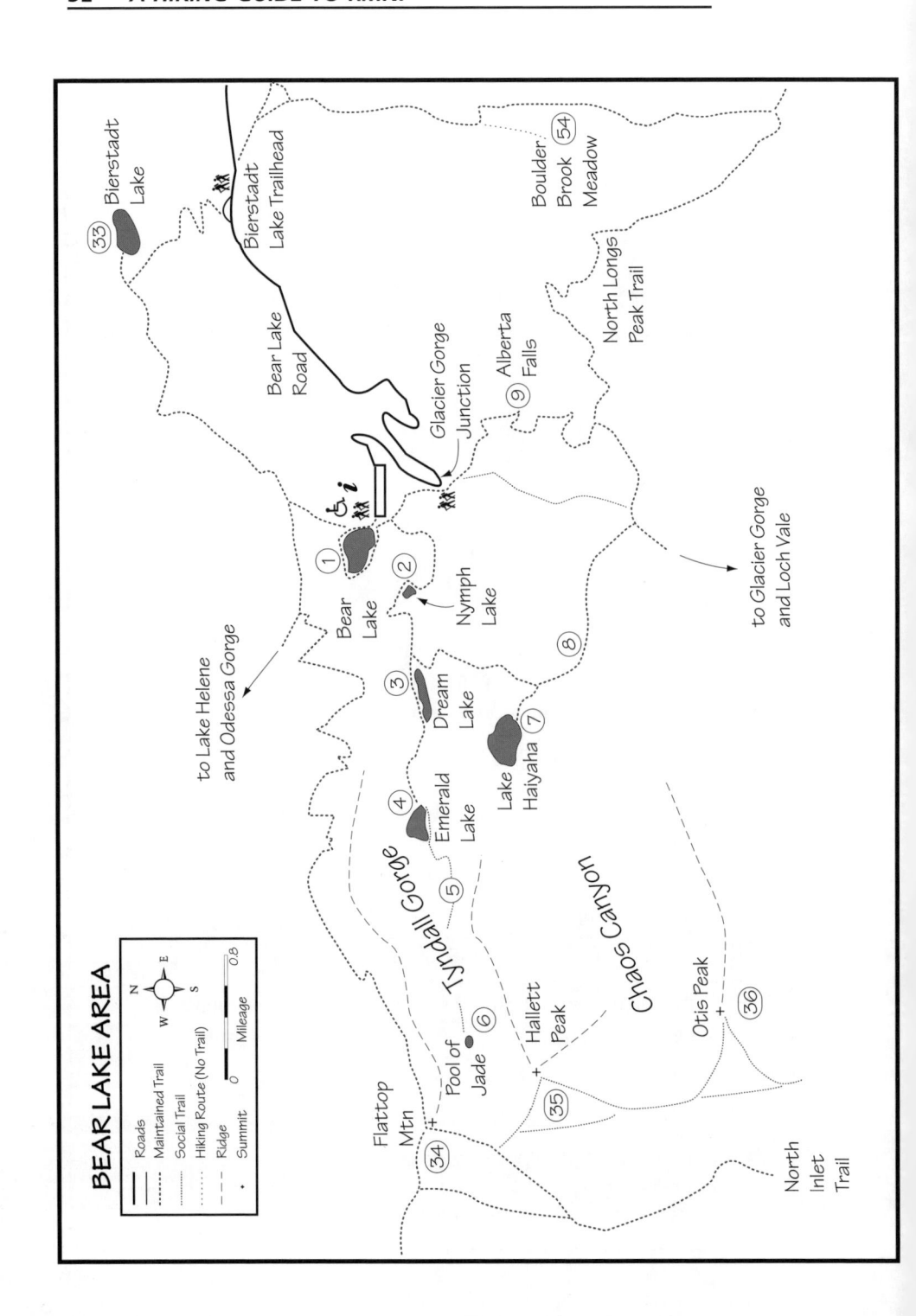

BEAR LAKE TRAILHEAD (II)

The following fifteen hikes are located to the north and west of Bear Lake. Hikes that go south and west can be found starting on Page 9.

33 BIERSTADT LAKE

Distance	Altitude	Elevation Gain	Difficulty
1.5 miles	9,400 ft	300 ft	easy

Maps: 10, 32, 48, 88. Starting at Bear Lake, take the Flattop trail uphill for about half a mile to a trail branching off to the right to Bierstadt Lake, less than another mile gently downhill. The lake is nestled in trees at the top of Bierstadt Moraine, with a great view of the Front Range. After lunch on its shore, you can continue downhill (about 1.5 miles) to the shuttle bus parking lot off Bear Lake Road, hopping a bus back to Bear Lake. Or you can walk around the lake to a trail that goes down (also about 1.5 miles) to the Bierstadt Lake trailhead on Bear Lake Road, again boarding a bus back to Bear Lake. In any case (unless you prefer working uphill to strolling downhill), the route from Bear Lake is the best choice among the several ways to reach Bierstadt Lake. In the winter it is a good snowshoe trek, but of course there is no bus—you will want to return the way you came.

34 FLATTOP MOUNTAIN

Distance	Altitude	Elevation Gain	Difficulty
4.5 miles	12,324 ft	2,800 ft	moderate

Maps: 8, 10, 32, 34, 88. Start at Bear Lake, taking the Flattop trail past the Bierstadt Lake turnoff (No. 33) to a second fork about a half-mile farther on. The right branch goes to Lake Helene (No. 37, page 35), while the main trail turns left, up through a young forest, past the Dream Lake and Emerald Lake overlooks, and finally rising to the flats that pass for a top. Keep going.

> LECTOR: This is not a lunch spot?
>
> AUCTOR: If you want to eat here, we recommend packaged crackers and cheese and diet cola.
>
> LECTOR: It looks to me like false advertising.
>
> AUCTOR: Why do you say that?
>
> LECTOR: Your book has fewer lunch spots than it claims.
>
> AUCTOR: Some are not numbered.

34 *A HIKING GUIDE TO RMNP*

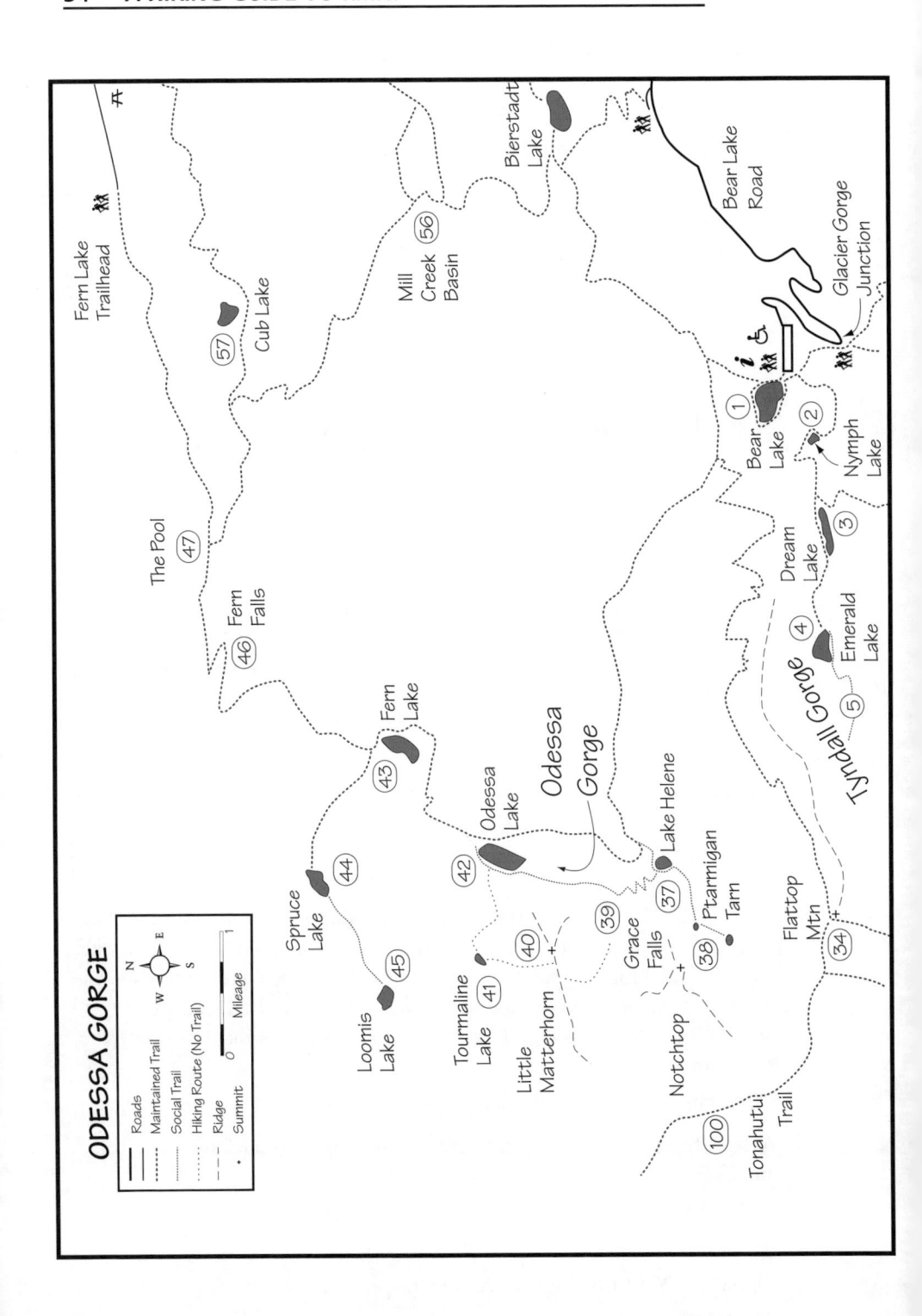

35 HALLETT PEAK

Distance	Altitude	Elevation Gain	Difficulty
5 miles	12,713 ft	3,200 ft	moderate

Maps: 8, 10, 32. From Flattop Mountain (No. 34) it is a short walk (south) around the top of Tyndall Glacier to the base of Hallett's western slope. A strenuous but uncomplicated bout of rock-hopping brings you to the top, where wonderful views may persuade you to stop for lunch. Unless you are going on, that is.

36 OTIS PEAK

Distance	Altitude	Elevation Gain	Difficulty
6 miles	12,486 ft	from Bear Lake 3,000 ft	hard

Maps: 8, 10, 32. From Hallett Peak (No. 35) you can descend south to the flats and then continue along the Continental Divide to Otis Peak. The loss of altitude involved in climbing both Hallett and Otis is tiring, but not seriously so. In fact we recommend what we call the Grand Slam (Flattop, Hallett, Otis, and Taylor), returning via Andrews Glacier to the Glacier Gorge parking lot. (See No. 16, page 21, which describes the more direct route to Taylor going *up* the glacier.) This foursome is seriously tiring, but lunch somewhere along the way refreshes body and soul.

37 LAKE HELENE

Distance	Altitude	Elevation Gain	Difficulty
3 miles	10,600 ft	1,100 ft	moderate

Map: 34. Take the Flattop trail from Bear Lake, continuing past the Bierstadt Lake turnoff (No. 33) to the next fork in the trail (see No. 34). The right branch goes west over gentle terrain for nearly two miles to a viewpoint above Odessa Lake (No. 42, page 38). Rather than continuing down the main trail into the Odessa valley, turn left at this point to approach Lake Helene along an unimproved path (heading toward Notchtop Mountain). It is only a hundred yards or so to the lake, which is a charming spot for lunch.

38 PTARMIGAN TARN

Distance	Altitude	Elevation Gain	Difficulty
3.5 miles	11,200 ft	1,700 ft	hard

Map: 34. Our son Bernard told us about this nameless tarn—we named it. Some route-finding and scrambling are needed to reach it. From the Lake Helene outlet (No. 37), follow the path along the west shore of the lake. Heading southwest toward the large snowfield between Flattop and Notchtop, climb up the ridge that leads to the shelf on which the tarn lies (hidden from view until you top out on the shelf). Try to avoid the krummholz that seems to bar the way up, negotiating the rocks instead. A short stretch of level tundra brings you to the tarn, with the awesome east face of Notchtop looming above (on the right). There is another tarn a short distance ahead (again invisible until you are almost there), but it is not the equal of the lower one, which is spectacularly lovely.

A strenuous way out is to follow the main outlet (next to Notchtop) to the top of Grace Falls. Do not attempt to climb down the rocks close to the falls! You can descend to the Odessa valley by hiking southeast to Lake Helene and then down the main trail, or (harder) by contouring northwest over the rocks and down next to a snowfield. Do not go on the snowfield itself unless you are sure it is not icy.

39 GRACE FALLS

Distance	Altitude	Elevation Gain	Difficulty
from Bear Lake 3.5 miles	10,300 ft	from Bear Lake 1,100 ft	hard

Map: 34. If you are interested in the top of this lovely waterfall, you can contour west from Lake Helene (No. 37) until you strike the Ptarmigan Tarn outlet (No. 38), then follow it down to the falls. A route to the bottom of the falls (more scenic) continues on the unimproved trail that brought you to Lake Helene. It soon turns downhill, and switchbacks into Odessa Gorge (past columbines if the season is right). The path is easy to lose as it steepens, dangerous if the slope is still a patchwork of snow. Later in the summer it is a scramble down through jumbled boulders, an effort richly rewarded by lunch close to the bottom of the falls.

40 THE LITTLE MATTERHORN

Distance	Altitude	Elevation Gain	Difficulty
from Bear Lake 4.5 miles	11,586 ft	from Bear Lake 2,100 ft	very hard

Map: 34. This is not for the faint-hearted. Hike to Lake Helene (No. 37) and descend to the bottom of Grace Falls as described in No. 39. Contour around the valley to its west side, then climb up the rocky slope to the top of the ridge that connects the Little Matterhorn to the main wall of the Continental Divide. Follow the ridge east as best you can (avoiding excessive exposure) toward the "top" of the Little Matterhorn. (The top is the end of the ridge, actually lower than some points behind it.)

A route that avoids loss of altitude is to contour around Odessa Gorge (from Lake Helene) *above* Grace Falls. The climb up to the Little Matterhorn ridge is then easier.

We have never made it to the top, for the last part of the ridge is dangerous without a rope. But there are good perches among the rocks for having a stomach-wrenching lunch. Then descend the north flank of the Little Matterhorn into Tourmaline Gorge. There is no easy way down—caution is the word. Exit via Tourmaline Lake (No. 41) and down the outlet to Odessa Lake. The best way out from there is described in No. 42.

41 TOURMALINE LAKE

Distance	Altitude	Elevation Gain	Difficulty
from Bear Lake 4.5 miles	10,600 ft	from Bear Lake 1,100 ft	moderate to hard

Map: 34. If the Little Matterhorn is included (No. 40), this hike is very hard. Tourmaline Lake itself, however, is more easily approached by hiking to Odessa Lake (No. 42) and going *up* the outlet, which flows into Odessa less than halfway around the west shore of the lake. Tourmaline Gorge is beautiful, and its lake (above treeline) is a lovely place to have lunch, but there is no trail worthy of the name. Keep the stream within earshot as you work up through the woods.

Some people climb the Little Matterhorn from Tourmaline Lake. We prefer the approach from Lake Helene.

42 ODESSA LAKE

Distance	Altitude	Elevation Gain	Difficulty
from Bear Lake 4 miles	10,000 ft	from Bear Lake 1,100 ft	moderate

Map: 34, 88. Many folks hike to Odessa Lake uphill, starting at the Fern Lake trailhead (see No. 57, p. 51) and returning the same way. The distance is 4.5 miles and the elevation gain is 1,900 ft. It is easier (and shorter) to start at Bear Lake and hike toward Lake Helene (No. 37, page 35). When you reach the viewpoint above Odessa Gorge, stay on the main trail, which heads down toward Odessa Lake. Then follow the spur that goes back a quarter-mile to the north shore of the lake. You will be rewarded by a magnificent view of Notchtop Mountain, Grace Falls, and the Little Matterhorn. There are lovely spots for lunch along the west shore of the lake, especially where the Tourmaline Lake outlet comes in (No. 41), and at the southern end, where a grassy (sometimes swampy) area beckons with its luminous green.

More adventurous souls may prefer the faint path from Lake Helene described in No. 39. That will bring you down into Odessa Gorge below Grace Falls. To reach the southern end of Odessa Lake (where the grassy area is), you must rediscover the trail you may have lost among the rocks higher up, or follow the stream that flows into the lake. Either way is a wilderness experience—and there are wonderful lunch spots everywhere.

You still have to hike out. Follow the trail around the west side of Odessa Lake and out the spur to the freeway. Here you have two choices. You can go back to Bear Lake via Lake Helene, a distance of about four miles (mostly downhill after you have hiked up to the Odessa Gorge overlook). It is more interesting (and not much farther) to head down the freeway to the Fern Lake parking lot. Of course that raises the question of how to get back to your car at Bear Lake. See No. 43.

LECTOR: You don't mind people, but you call their trail a freeway.

AUCTOR: No criticism intended. I like freeways.

43 FERN LAKE

Distance	Altitude	Elevation Gain	Difficulty
from Bear Lake 4.5 miles	9,500 ft	from Bear Lake 1,100 ft	moderate

Map: 34. This beautiful lake is about a half-mile down the trail from Odessa Lake (No. 42). Or you can hike *up* from the Fern Lake trailhead, at the end of a spur off the Bear Lake Road (see No. 57, page 51). The distance is only 4 miles this way, but the elevation gain is 1,400 ft.

There is a ranger cabin nestled in the trees on the northwest side of the lake. When my mother belonged to the Colorado Mountain Club (before the Park was born in 1915), she would ride a horse to Fern Lake, and stay overnight at the lodge there. Later it fell into disrepair, its last indignity coming at the hands of Park personnel who burned down what was left of it. One time we were hiking past the ruins and met a ranger, who described its demise. He seemed unconcerned that a historic landmark had been destroyed, evidently preferring a "return to nature," as they describe these things. Are we not part of nature, too, with all our works? Why does a beaver house qualify and a human habitation does not?

LECTOR: That's sophistry.

AUCTOR: You haven't answered the question.

LECTOR: Nature is defined to mean the world apart from man.

AUCTOR: Not in my dictionary it isn't.

44 SPRUCE LAKE

Distance	Altitude	Elevation Gain	Difficulty
4.5 miles	9,700 ft	1,500 ft	moderate

Map: 34. Hike to Fern Lake (No. 43) by the shortest route (starting at the Fern Lake trailhead – see No. 57, page 51). Just below the patrol cabin an unimproved trail branches off from the freeway, heading for Spruce Lake a half-mile away. The woods are lovely and the lake is serene, just the place for hungry hikers. Castle Rock and Stones Peak rise dramatically above the lake.

45 LOOMIS LAKE

Distance	Altitude	Elevation Gain	Difficulty
5 miles	10,200 ft	2,100 ft	hard

Map: 34. Hike to Spruce Lake (No. 44) by the shortest route (starting at the Fern Lake trailhead—see No. 57, page 51). If you are willing to postpone gastronomic gratification for a higher end, follow the steep trail up the inlet, or (if you lose it) bushwhack to Loomis Lake. It's worth the trouble. About half a mile (beyond Spruce Lake) and you're there, above the trees and seemingly within easy reach of the Continental Divide. Leave it to heaven and have lunch.

46 FERN FALLS

Distance	Altitude	Elevation Gain	Difficulty
2.5 miles	8,800 ft	600 ft	moderate

Map: 34. If you have come from Bear Lake via Lake Helene and Odessa Lake (No. 37, page 35 and No. 42, page 38), this spot is at 6 miles and on your way down. The direct route is 2.5 miles *up,* from the Fern Lake trailhead (see No. 57, page 51). Either way it is a truly classic lunch spot. (It often appears that many other people agree.) Between the falls and The Pool (No. 47) you may notice (if you are listening) a stretch of trail where the balance control is set for stereo sound from two streams, Fern Creek on one side and Spruce Creek on the other. Leonard Bernstein could not arrange his orchestra better.

LECTOR: Leonard Bernstein did not arrange his orchestra at all.

AUCTOR: I meant Leopold Stokowski.

47 THE POOL

Distance	Altitude	Elevation Gain	Difficulty
2 miles	8,400 ft	200 ft	easy

Map: 34. Like Fern Falls (No. 46) this spot is on the way down if you started at Bear Lake. Of course the obvious way to reach it is from the other direction. In any case, this is where the Big Thompson River, plunging down from its source in Forest Canyon, has scoured the rock walls in a good imitation of a circular bowl. It looks uncommonly like a swimming hole, except that the swirling current is too violent for that. Have lunch instead.

Between the Pool and the Fern Lake trailhead you will pass through the remarkable Arch Rocks, looking for all the world like something the Druids arranged. Speaking of arrangements: if you are going downhill on the nine-mile trek that started at Bear Lake, you will have already planned a way to get back to your car at Bear Lake.

LECTOR: You didn't say anything about that until now.

AUCTOR: It pays to browse through the book before you hike nine miles from your car.

LECTOR: You're going to make me walk from here?

AUCTOR: Fortunately there's a shuttle bus to Bear Lake, if the time and season are right.

LECTOR: What if they aren't?

AUCTOR: You might try hitchhiking. The easiest arrangement, however, is to park one car at Bear Lake and bring another to the Fern Lake trailhead.

LECTOR: I haven't mastered the trick of driving two cars at once.

AUCTOR: I was assuming you don't do these epics alone.

Finger Food Delight
Di Batten, Tasmania Australia

Tom Thumb tomatoes
Lebanese flat bread
White Castello or hummus
Celery sticks

Watermelon and Mango with Lime
Carol Abernathy, North Carolina

1 4-lb. Piece watermelon
2 mangoes, peeled, pitted, and cut into 1-inch chunks
Add fresh lime juice to taste
1 teaspoon grated lime zest
½ teaspoon sugar

Toss together all ingredients. Cover and chill. Stir a couple times over 20 minutes. Place in something that can insulate and place deep in your pack to preserve chill.

42   A HIKING GUIDE TO RMNP

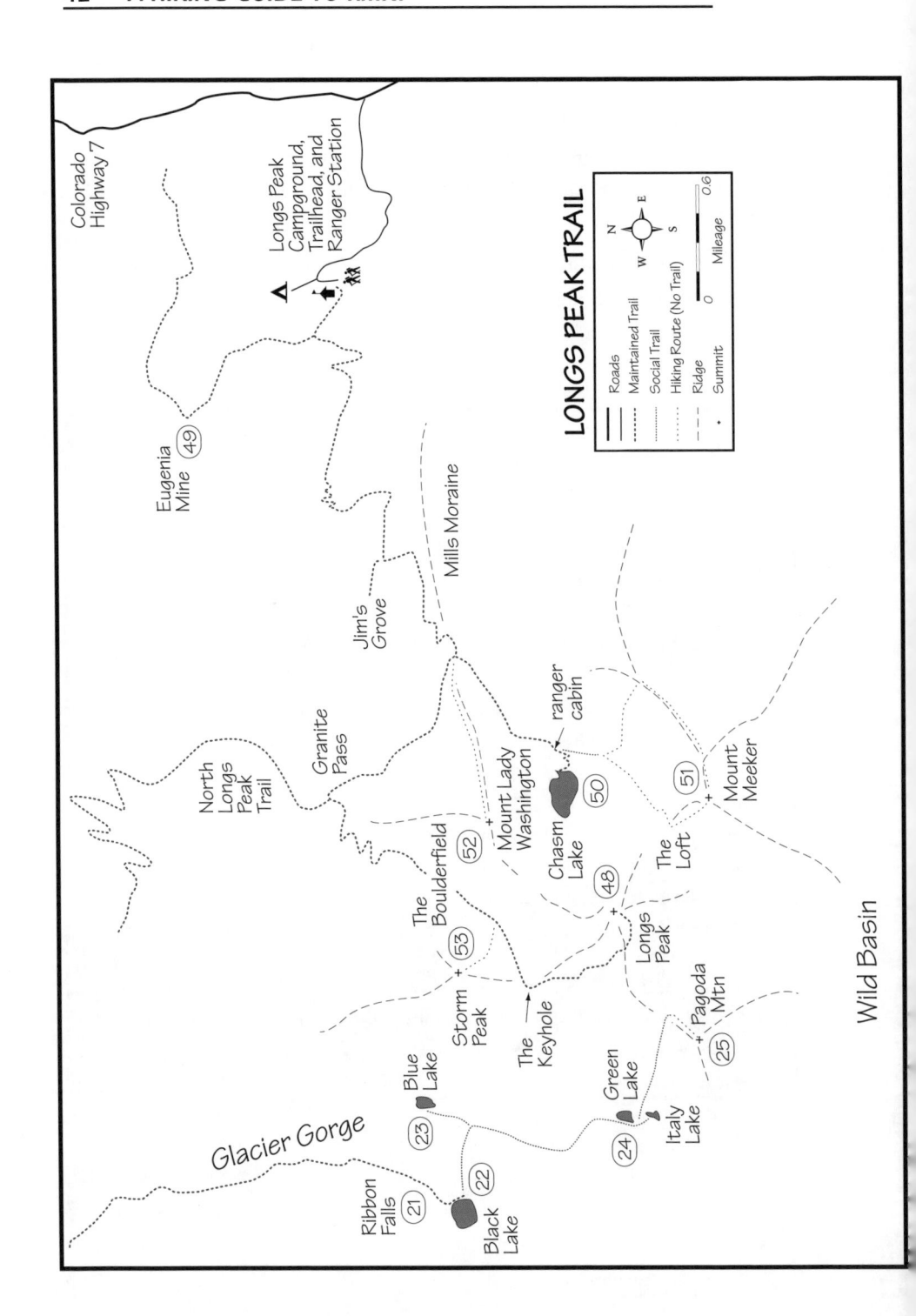

LONGS PEAK TRAILHEAD

48 LONGS PEAK

Distance	Altitude	Elevation Gain	Difficulty
8 miles	14,255 ft	4,900 ft	very hard

Maps: 16, 42, 81. Drive up Colorado 7 from Estes Park about 7.5 miles and turn west on the road that goes uphill for another mile to the Longs Peak ranger station and trailhead. There are many ways to get to the top of this famous fourteener, all but one being too hard for inclusion in a book on lunch spots. Even the regular route is a technical climb for most of the year—check with the Park Service if there is any doubt whether it is open for ordinary hikers. It is close to technical on the best of days, which is why the peak is such an attractive climb. It is no slog, but a genuine challenge—a memorable experience by any standard.

You should start well before sunrise, to give yourself ample time to get to the top and off again before the usual afternoon storms move in. The trail from the ranger station to the Boulderfield (six miles) is easy, provided you have done the preliminary hikes most people need if they are to avoid lung-popping weariness. Turn around if you find the effort too tiring, or the weather threatening, and come back another day. Assuming you are enjoying the hike, prepare for a climb when you head for the Keyhole. This fabled formation (looking its name) is at the low point of the ridge between Longs Peak and Storm Peak (No. 53), less than a half-mile west of the Boulderfield horse rack.

Rock-hopping changes to climbing as you approach the shelter cabin just below the Keyhole. This little hut was built to commemorate Agnes Vaille, who died on a winter climb of the east face of Longs Peak in 1925. My mother and aunt, both members of the Colorado Mountain Club somewhat earlier, knew Miss Vaille, but did not share her ambition to climb the peak in all seasons. Her story is an interesting and tragic epic, but it is more edifying to move up to the Keyhole and be struck dumb by the spectacular scenery that is so sudden as to be gut-wrenching. Glacier Gorge is spread out below, with all the surrounding peaks across the void. (See Black Lake, No. 22, page 24, for their names and location.)

After the Keyhole, the route (marked by orange and red "targets" or "eggs") wanders purposefully across the Ledges toward the Trough, frustrating the tired hiker by detours that avoid exposure on the steep slabs above Glacier

Gorge. At one point there are two iron spikes cemented into the rock, to help negotiate some unavoidable exposure—hikers are sometimes spooked by these, but they look worse than they are. The Trough is actually more of a hazard, due to rocks dislodged by hikers above. If you hear anybody yell "ROCK," it is prudent to duck.

The top of the Trough can be tough to manage, especially if it is wet or icy. But the view into Wild Basin is exhilarating, and the rest of the climb is worth whatever effort it requires. The immediate problem is a level (but intimidating) section called the Narrows, which I first saw at age 12 with my mother as guide, informing her that it was time to turn around—she persuaded me to continue, a decision that marked the beginning of a life-long love affair with mountains.

Climbing another corner at the end of the Narrows, the hiker is confronted with the final test: the steep slabs of the Homestretch. These are not hard to climb, but they require care coming back down, and are dangerous in rain or snow. That is one reason why it is important to get off the top before bad weather sets in (the other being the threat of lightning). Assuming the sun is still shining, and you feel like eating lunch, you may want to look around for a shady spot. There being none, you might enjoy the southwest corner of the football field that is the top. Not too close to the edge, however, or you might drop your sandwich (worse yet, your thermos) on climbers in the Trough below.

Our children, who explored Longs Peak at an early age (against their better judgment), did not seem as interested in lunch as in sleep when they reached the top. This condition is not uncommon—in fact some people are even more interested in getting down. My wife is of this persuasion. She is an accomplished climber, but five minutes after success she is pointing out clouds on the horizon that she claims will shortly be dumping snow on the entire Front Range. Occasionally she is right—we have descended the Homestretch more than once when it was too slippery to be safe.

Our youngest two (Robert and Mary) went up the cable route on the north face when they were five and seven, respectively. The cable had long been removed, which meant that we needed ropes. The friends who provided them saw us safely up the technical section, and then went ahead to organize a *claque* at the top. When Robert and Mary topped out, a chorus of applause, which naturally warmed their hearts, greeted them.

But we list this lunch spot with a *caveat*. There are better places to eat, not the least of which is the shelter hut at the Keyhole. Lacking any vestige of elegance, it is nonetheless a reassuring stop in a storm. Better yet, get off the peak altogether, waiting for lunch until you are back in the trees along Alpine Brook.

49 EUGENIA MINE

Distance	Altitude	Elevation Gain	Difficulty
1.5 miles	9,900 ft	500 ft	easy

Maps: 42, 78. Hike up the Longs Peak trail to the first fork (about half a mile from the trailhead). The right-hand branch goes on for a mile to Inn Brook, where lie the remains of Eugenia Mine. You can stop here for lunch, or continue a short distance to Moore Park, a lovely meadow below the junction of this trail and the old Storm Pass trail (see No. 86, page 79).

50 CHASM LAKE

Distance	Altitude	Elevation Gain	Difficulty
4 miles	11,800 ft	2,400 ft	hard

Maps: 16, 42, 81. Follow the Longs Peak trail for about three miles to the fork at the top of Mills Moraine. The left branch goes to Chasm Lake, taking off toward the magnificent cirque bounded by Mt. Meeker, Longs Peak, and Mt. Lady Washington (from left to right). If the snow slope below the cliffs of Lady Washington is still there, cross it cautiously, pause to appreciate Peacock Pool (below, on your left) and Columbine Falls (across the way), walk through the lovely meadow with the patrol cabin at its far end, and climb up the rocky gully to the shelf overlooking Chasm Lake.

The east face of Longs rises unbelievably above the lake, with technical climbers scaling the vertical part (the Diamond) on almost every summer day. Following their progress, however, is like watching paint dry. The reason for coming is to enjoy a classic lunch at one of the most spectacular places in the Park. Don't allow the marmots to steal your food.

51 MOUNT MEEKER

Distance	Altitude	Elevation Gain	Difficulty
5.5 miles	13,911 ft	4,500	very hard

Maps: 16, 42, 81. There are two good routes up this second-highest peak in the Park (which few people climb, because it is just short of a fourteener). One way is to turn left from the meadow below Chasm Lake (No. 50) and labor up the scree slope (through the "Iron Gates" on the left) to the east ridge of Meeker. Turn right and follow the ridge as it rises to the east summit. You will then perceive that the true top is the west summit, reached by a knife edge that requires care. There is barely room at the top for one person to have lunch—others may gather round a few feet below. The view of Longs Peak is unusual.

The other way up Meeker also starts in the meadow below Chasm Lake, but goes southwest to the Loft between Longs and Meeker. Avoid the cliffs on the way up by finding the Ramp to their left, a ledge that looks worse than it is. Turn left at the Loft and climb up the unremarkable ridge (except for a boulder problem at the top) to the west summit of Meeker.

After lunch on your airy perch, you must still get down. Neither route is attractive in reverse—the knife edge to the false summit seems more forbidding than on the way up, and the Ramp below the Loft is easy to miss. Unless you are an experienced route-finder, Meeker is best left for another time.

52 MOUNT LADY WASHINGTON

Distance	Altitude	Elevation Gain	Difficulty
5.5 miles	13,281 ft	3,900 ft	hard

Maps: 16, 42. After the Chasm Lake cut-off (No. 50), the Longs Peak trail goes northwest along the base of Mt. Lady Washington. Turn up the rocky slope at almost any point to climb to the east (false) summit. Or wait until the lower part of the Boulderfield, from which you can climb directly to the west (true) summit. Each offers a superb view of the east face of Longs Peak.

53 STORM PEAK

Distance	Altitude	Elevation Gain	Difficulty
6.5 miles	13,326 ft	3,900 ft	hard

Maps: 16, 42. From the Boulderfield (see No. 48, page 43) it is not far to the top of Storm Peak (to the right of the Keyhole), but the climb is over jumbled rocks. Perhaps it is not worthwhile for its own sake, but the view of the north face of Longs Peak is unusual, especially in early summer when it is still white with snow. As you top out, the sudden panorama of peaks surrounding Glacier Gorge (spread out below) is even more astonishing than at the Keyhole. Lunch is more satisfying, too, because the next part of the hike is down.

> LECTOR: May we skip all these alpine ascents? Peak-bagging is for the birds.

AUCTOR: They do seem to enjoy it.

LECTOR: Only a bird would be interested in this perch.

AUCTOR: It seems that one has already made off with part of your lunch.

Banana Nut Bread and Cappuccino
Bill Webster, North Carolina

You'll need:

1 cup Jiffy mix
1 cup sugar
2 eggs
¾ cup milk
3-4 mushed-up bananas
1 cup chopped nuts (walnuts and/or pecans work best)

Mix all ingredients then pour into greased pans. Bake at 350 degrees for about one hour. Drop into a zip-lock bag and pack on the top of your daypack! Take along some butter in one of those little plastic storage containers.

The bread is a meal by itself but don't forget to buy some of those bottled cappuccino drinks that can be bought at any food store. Transfer the drinks to a plastic water bottle and refrigerate before the hike.

48 *A HIKING GUIDE TO RMNP*

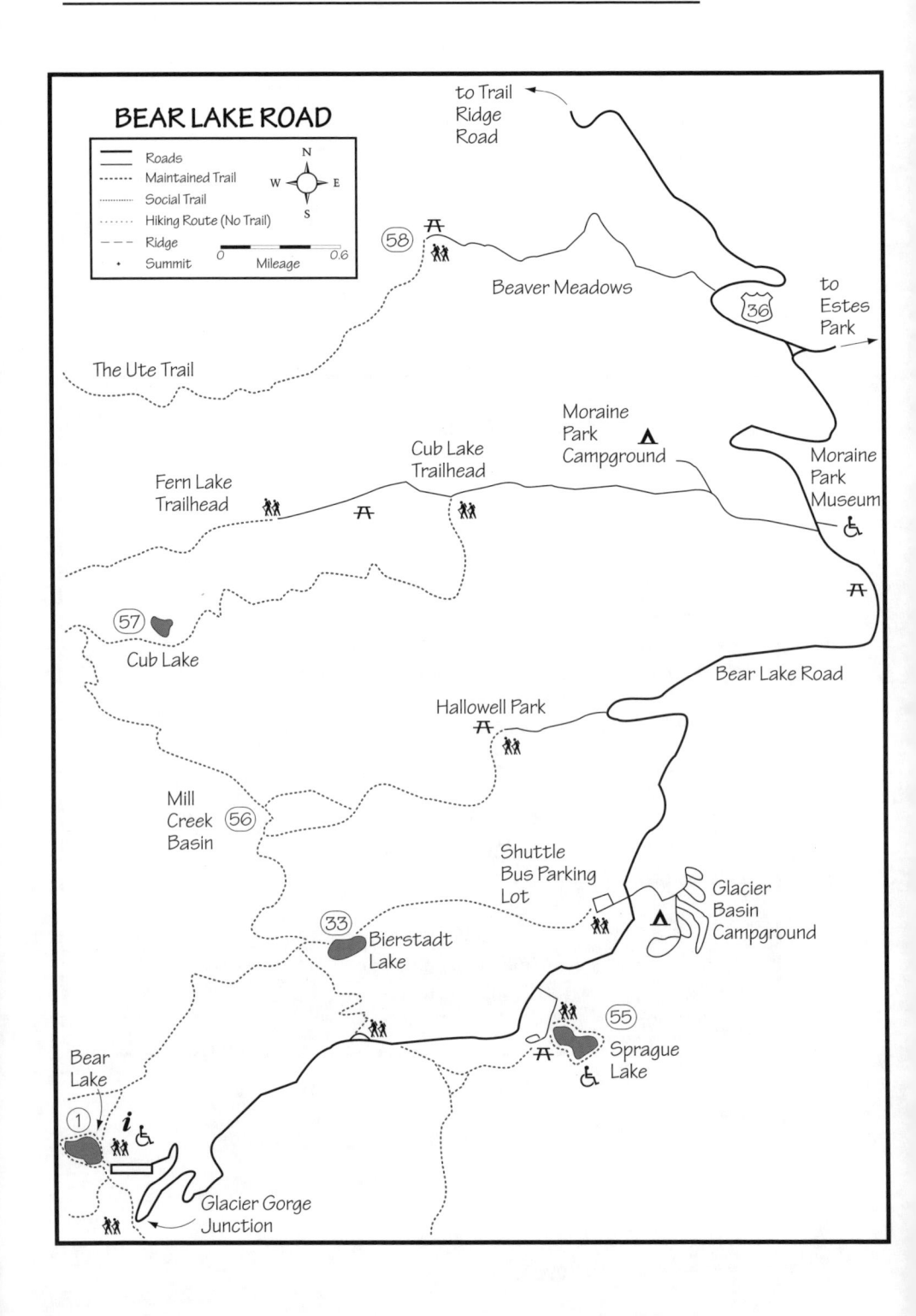

BEAR LAKE ROAD TRAILHEADS

54 BOULDER BROOK MEADOW

Distance	Altitude	Elevation Gain	Difficulty
2 miles	9,500 ft	700 ft	moderate

Maps: 10, 32, 78, 88. Park at the Bierstadt Lake trailhead on Bear Lake Road (the early bird finds a space, others may have to use the shuttle bus). Cross the road and follow the Storm Pass trail leading gently downhill (southeast) to Glacier Brook. Cross the bridge and continue south, ignoring the trails that branch off uphill (west) and downhill (east). After a quarter-mile or so, there should be a sign (among others) that says Boulder Brook and points south, which now begins to be uphill—steeply uphill for a while, until you reach the first bridge over Boulder Brook. Continue past the second bridge to the third bridge.

At this point (instead of crossing the bridge) leave the trail and follow the stream uphill until you reach the meadow—past uneven turf that broadens into a lovely area of deep grass next to Boulder Brook. You have surely brought a beverage to put into the stream until it is ice-cold. Lie down in the grass (feet toward the stream) and study the sky. Look south to see Longs Peak and Storm Peak looming over the valley. Behind you is an aspen-studded hill that you may want to climb if you are more ambitious than we are.

After no less than an hour enjoying lunch in this fair glade, hike slowly down the trail, stopping often to drink in the beauty of Boulder Brook (not literally—you might get the Rocky Mountain glitch). It is our favorite stream, unspoiled by natural or unnatural catastrophe, with greener edges and more sparkling waterfalls than most anywhere else in the Park. (You may disagree with our *obiter dicta* concerning such matters. But presumably you bought this book as a guide to classic lunch spots. Trust us.)

Another way to reach the Boulder Brook meadow is up the Alberta Falls trail from the Glacier Gorge parking lot (see No. 9, page 17), hiking about a mile past the falls to a fork in the trail. The right branch (heavily traveled) is the main trail to the junction of Glacier Gorge and Loch Vale. The left branch descends to a bridge over Glacier Creek and then rises for several miles to Granite Pass below the Boulderfield (where Boulder Brook starts). My parents used to climb Longs Peak by this route (sometimes called the North Longs Peak trail). Now it is seldom used for that purpose.

Follow the left branch as it climbs east and southeast past Half Mountain. About a mile from the bridge you will see a sign marking the top of the Boulder Brook trail, which descends north to the meadow already described. It is not easy to see the meadow when you are going downhill toward the third bridge from the bottom (nor is it reasonable to expect that you can count bridges in reverse order). Perhaps it is best not to choose this approach until you have found the meadow from the other direction. Moreover, it will bring you out at the Bierstadt Lake parking lot, and your car is up the road at the Glacier Gorge lot (or even at Bear Lake, if congestion forced you there). You may need a bus.

55 SPRAGUE LAKE CIRCUIT

Distance	Altitude	Elevation Gain	Difficulty
0.5 miles	8,700 ft	0	trivial

Maps: 48, 78. This popular lake is two minutes off Bear Lake Road, not far above the shuttle bus parking lot. There is a trail around it that can be negotiated by people confined to wheelchairs. A huge blue spruce tree at its northern end is one of the finest specimens we have seen anywhere. There are splendid views of the Front Range. A short distance west of the lake there are picnic tables and a brook that small children can dabble in. Trails go off in several directions. As a family lunch spot it can hardly be excelled. Of course many visitors to the Park enthusiastically agree, which might seem to limit your options. As we have pointed out before, however, you can find peace and quiet close by.

LECTOR: Now this is more my style.

AUCTOR: I thought it might be. You deserve a break.

LECTOR: Why do you think I have this cast on my leg?

56 MILL CREEK BASIN

Distance	Altitude	Elevation Gain	Difficulty
1.5 miles	9,000 ft	600 ft	easy

Maps: 34, 48. Drive up Bear Lake Road to the turn-off into Hollowell Park. At the end of this spur there are picnic tables next to Mill Creek (a family lunch spot like Sprague Lake, but less busy). If you feel like hiking, follow the trail west to Mill Creek Basin (taking the left branch at the fork about a mile from the trailhead). Much of the hike is along Mill Creek itself, and is very pleasant. The basin consists of a beautiful meadow surrounded by gentle hills, with a couple of backcountry campgrounds strategically located among the trees. After lunch walk north across the meadow until you meet a trail that goes left (northwest) toward Cub Lake. Go right instead, to head down (after a short rise) through a wonderful aspen grove to join the trail you came up.

Our young son Bernard claimed he would build a house among these aspen. Upon learning that the Park Service frowns on such projects, he abandoned the idea. Now he and his family use our house (in Estes Park, with a few aspen trees here and there) as a launching pad for expeditions into the Park.

57 CUB LAKE

Distance	Altitude	Elevation Gain	Difficulty
2.5 miles	8,600 ft	500 ft	easy

Maps: 34, 48. You can reach Cub Lake from Mill Creek Basin (No. 56). Your car, however, is back in Hollowell Park. It is easier to do another trip by driving to the Cub Lake trailhead. Follow the Bear Lake Road to the Moraine Park Campground exit, then take the left branch of the next fork in the road. The Cub Lake trailhead soon appears on the left side of the road (which continues to the Fern Lake parking lot). There is a nice lunch spot at the trailhead, next to a placid stream. The trail to Cub Lake is easy and peaceful, and the trees along the north shore provide shade for lunch. You can continue up the trail to the Pool (see No. 47, page 40) and hike out to the Fern Lake parking lot. But then you have to walk a mile back to your car.

LECTOR: The fault, dear Brutus, is not in our cars but in ourselves.

AUCTOR: There is a ride in the affairs of men, which taken at the bus stop, leads on to fortune.

LECTOR: We should go on the stage.

AUCTOR: There's one leaving in ten minutes.

52   A HIKING GUIDE TO RMNP

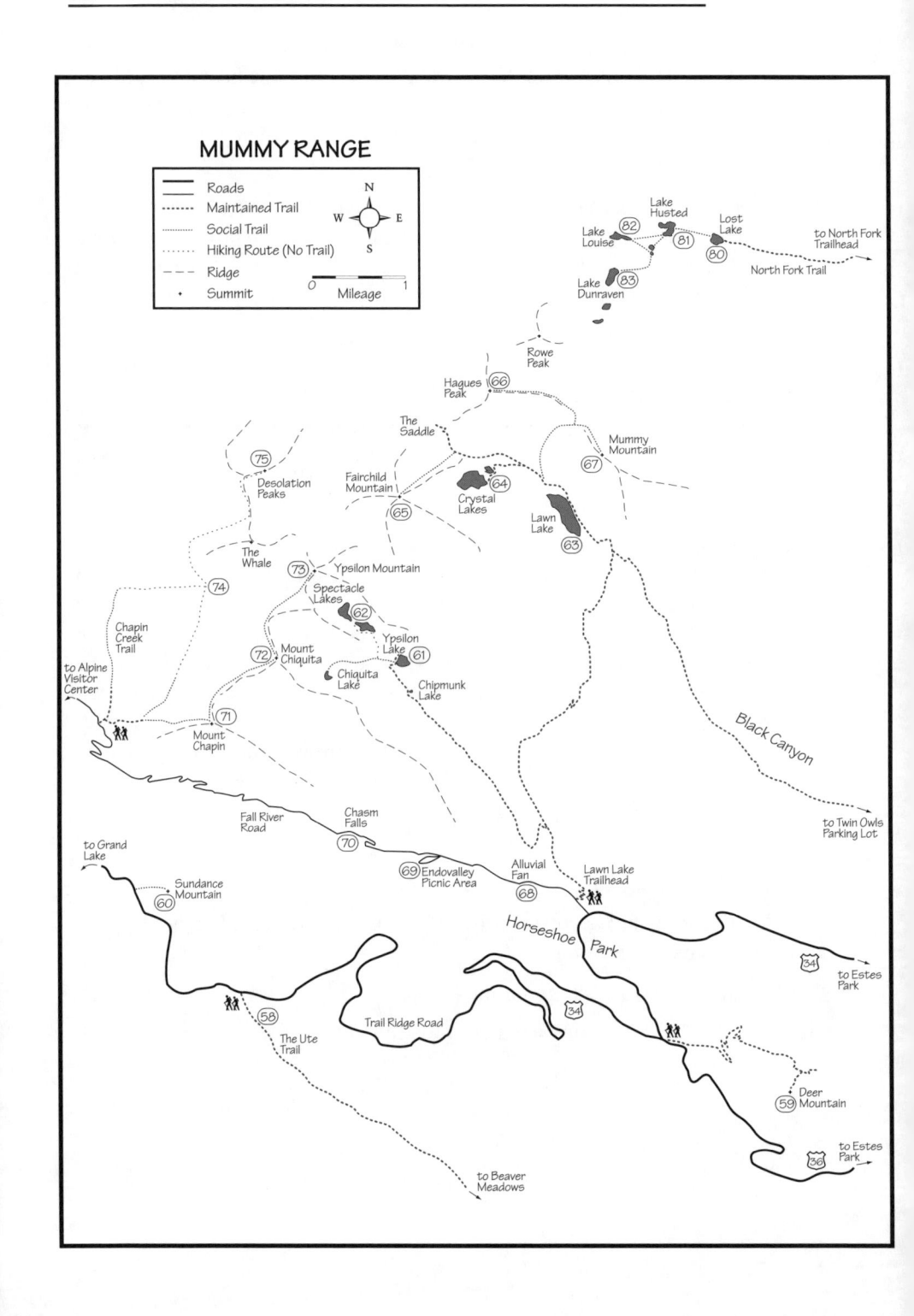

TRAIL RIDGE ROAD TRAILHEADS

58 THE UTE TRAIL

Distance	Altitude	Elevation Loss	Difficulty
6 miles down	11,400 ft	3,000 ft	moderate

Map: 48. This ancient way starts (or ends, depending on your point of view) in Beaver Meadows, at a trailhead reached by entering the Park on US 36, driving past the Bear Lake Road, and then (shortly) turning left on the spur to the trailhead. You will pass a helicopter pad, which is a staging area for many Park searches and rescues.

Picnic tables near Beaver Brook provide a good family lunch spot. Our advice is to putter around here, possibly walking up the trail a reasonable distance, and avoid the climb to Trail Ridge Road. Did we mention that the trail goes up that far, for six miles? Transportation back down can be arranged, or you can hike back on the same trail (but that means 12 miles). It is less painful to reverse your point of view.

Take *two* cars to the Beaver Meadows trailhead, park one, then drive up Trail Ridge Road to a small parking space about two miles above Rainbow Curve. (Be early, or no space will present itself.) The trail to Beaver Meadows starts here, meandering along Tombstone Ridge to Timberline Pass and down into Windy Gulch. There are several good places to stop for lunch as you descend. At one of them I stuck my old wooden ice axe into the ground before eating, then left without it. (I had brought it along because it was early in the summer, and the snow at Timberline Pass was steep.) When I realized next day that it was missing, I hiked back up to the spot from Beaver Meadows, but the axe was gone. I had a mournful lunch.

If you see anybody with a wooden ice axe (they are made of lighter metal now), ask where it came from. You might get an honest answer: "I found it on the Ute Trail twenty years ago." Please give the bearer my blessing. When people take things not their own, it may be due to a need greater than the owner's. Or so the parable goes. My own view is somewhat stricter.

59 DEER MOUNTAIN

Distance	Altitude	Elevation Gain	Difficulty
3 miles	10,013 ft	1,100 ft	moderate

Map: 72. Enter the Park on US 36 and drive past the Bear Lake Road and the Beaver Meadows spur (No. 58) to the junction with US 34 on Deer Ridge (or take US 34 from Estes Park to this point). The Deer Mountain trail starts just east of the junction, and meanders for three miles to the top. It is a courtesy to call this foothill a mountain, but the view from the top is first-rate.

LECTOR: Define "mountain."

AUCTOR: Well, it depends on where you are. In Rocky Mountain National Park I understand a mountain to be anything that rises above tree line. Estes Cone does (barely), Deer Mountain does not. Twin Sisters does, Lily Mountain does not. And so it goes.

LECTOR: Lily Mountain isn't in the Park.

AUCTOR: I'm glad to see you taking an interest in these details. Nevertheless I intend to list it.

60 SUNDANCE MOUNTAIN

Distance	Altitude	Elevation Gain	Difficulty
0.5 miles	12,466 ft	400 ft	easy

Map: none. This is but a half-mile walk-up from various parking spots on Trail Ridge Road (about a mile north and west of the Forest Canyon overlook). Because you will have done most of the altitude gain in a car, the 400-ft walk-up can be a shock to your system if you are not yet acclimated. Climb slowly, so that you will enjoy your lunch. The view down the Fall River drainage is salutary (as is the scenery in every direction).

LAWN LAKE TRAILHEAD

61 YPSILON LAKE

Distance	Altitude	Elevation Gain	Difficulty
4.5 miles	10,500 ft	2,000 ft	moderate

Maps: 52, 76. Enter the Park at the Fall River entrance on US 34, and drive past the sheep-viewing stretch to the Fall River Road, where it starts in Horseshoe Park. The Lawn Lake trailhead is almost immediately on the right. Follow the trail about a mile to the fork whose left branch crosses Roaring River. This is the way to Ypsilon Lake, some 3.5 miles farther (up a long ridge and down again past Chipmunk Lake). A good place to have lunch is at the inlet on the west side of the lake, where the visible trail ends. There is a nearly invisible path up the inlet, but that's another story. (See No. 62.)

62 SPECTACLE LAKES

Distance	Altitude	Elevation Gain	Difficulty
5 miles	11,400 ft	2,800 ft	hard

Map: 52. Unless you are an experienced route-finder, stopping at Ypsilon Lake (No. 61) is prudent. There is no easy way to these lakes that lie at the base of Mt. Ypsilon. You can try to follow the faint trail up the Ypsilon Lake inlet, but chances are it will disappear when you most need it. If you choose to go on, be prepared for steep climbs along waterfalls and exposed clambering up smooth slabs. In any case, turn right when the stream branches—the left branch comes down from Chiquita Lake.

Once my wife and I avoided the route up the inlet by hiking around the north side of Ypsilon Lake and heading up a scree slope to a ridge that took us west toward the lower Spectacle Lake. Unfortunately we arrived on top of a cliff that we didn't care to descend to the lake, and went back defeated.

Another time we went up the inlet with our youngest daughter Mary. What I chiefly remember is a layback above a waterfall that I thought might be the end of a happy career. My wife and daughter had already done it, and it was a question of following them or facing humiliation. (I recommend humiliation.)

The last time was three years ago, with son John and a rope. He found a route that was unexpectedly reasonable, and the rope never came out of his pack. But I'm not sure I could repeat it.

If you get there with sandwiches uncrushed and liquid containers intact, enjoy one of the most spectacular lunch spots in the Park.

63 LAWN LAKE

Distance	Altitude	Elevation Gain	Difficulty
6 miles	10,800 ft	2,200 ft	moderate to hard

Maps: 52, 72, 76. Back at the fork in the Lawn Lake trail (No. 61), take the right-hand branch on up to Lawn Lake, a long way from the trailhead on Fall River Road. There was once a dam at the southern end of the lake, but it broke in 1982, causing a catastrophic flood. One good result was the renewal of downtown Estes Park following the destruction (but that's like saying the San Francisco earthquake or the Chicago fire improved those communities).

Actually we have not been to Lawn Lake since the flood. I never thought highly of it as a lunch spot anyway, but now I am told it is more interesting. If you agree, I'm glad to have listed it.

64 CRYSTAL LAKES

Distance	Altitude	Elevation Gain	Difficulty
7.5 miles	11,500 ft	3,000 ft	hard

Map: 52. From Lawn Lake (No. 63) hike up along the inlet for a steep half-mile to a fork in the trail. The left branch eventually brings you to these lovely lakes above timberline, where the view and lunch are both pleasurable. Perhaps this is the time to bring out something elegant, like a bacon, lettuce, and tomato sandwich washed down by a good red wine. Red grapes will add to the festivity.

   LECTOR: What is this sudden flourish of red?

   AUCTOR: Would thy hand rather the multitudinous seas incarnadine?

   LECTOR: I thought we gave up quoting Shakespeare.

   AUCTOR: Only Hamlet, not Macbeth.

Hike #21 Ribbon Falls

Hike #30 Solitude Lake with Powell Peak in the background

Hike #98 Bluebird Lake

Hike #50 Chasm Lake with avalanche on the East Face of Long's Peak

Hike #25 Maria Gillet on the top of Pagoda Mountain with Long's Peak in the background

Hike #48 North Face of Long's Peak in summer conditions

Hike #3 Dream Lake with Hallett Peak in the background

Hike #13 Petit Grepon from Sky Pond

65 FAIRCHILD MOUNTAIN

Distance	Altitude	Elevation Gain	Difficulty
9 miles	13,502 ft	5,000 ft	hard

Map: 52. At the fork in the trail above Lawn Lake (see No. 64), take the right branch toward the Saddle between Fairchild Mountain (left) and Hagues Peak (right). Rather than continuing to the Saddle itself, climb the higher part of the ridge to its left, turning southwest to go up the summit slope of Fairchild. The view in every direction is wonderful. But it's a weary slog (greater distance and elevation gain than Longs Peak!).

66 HAGUES PEAK

Distance	Altitude	Elevation Gain	Difficulty
9 miles	13,560 ft	5,000 ft	hard

Map: 52. About halfway between Lawn Lake and Crystal Lakes (No. 64) turn right to climb up to the saddle between Hagues Peak (left) and Mummy Mountain (right). Then turn left to reach the top of Hagues. It is the fourth-highest point in the Park (behind Longs, Meeker, and Chiefs Head)—a great place for lunch, but like Fairchild a greater distance and elevation gain than Longs Peak.

LECTOR: Your use of capitals (Saddle versus saddle) is eccentric.

AUCTOR: Why didn't you complain when you climbed up the Ramp to the Loft, or hiked past the Pool?

LECTOR: There was only one of each.

AUCTOR: Blame the US Geological Survey.

67 MUMMY MOUNTAIN

Distance	Altitude	Elevation Gain	Difficulty
8 miles	13,425 ft	4,900 ft	hard

Maps: 52, 72. From the saddle (not the Saddle) between Hagues and Mummy (No. 66), turn right instead of left. The top of Mummy Mountain is another good lunch spot (only eight miles from the car).

FALL RIVER ROAD TRAILHEADS

68 ALLUVIAL FAN

Distance	Altitude	Elevation Gain	Difficulty
0	8,500 ft	0	none

Map: 52. Continuing on the Fall River Road beyond the Lawn Lake trailhead (see No. 61, page 55), you will soon come to the awesome debris brought down by Roaring River when the Lawn Lake dam broke in 1982—not a bad place to park, putter, and have lunch. The enormous boulders scattered around are testimony to the force of water pouring down a narrow channel. Less obvious, but still remarkable, is the small lake formed by the rubble damming the Fall River (a short distance southwest of the bridge over Roaring River). The Park Service has predicted that the lake will gradually drain away, but as of this writing it is still there.

A largely unsung hero of the flood is the trash collector who saw it coming and alerted the authorities. He saved the lives of campers downstream, and made it possible for the town of Estes Park to brace for the deluge that came roaring down the main street.

69 ENDOVALLEY PICNIC AREA

Distance	Altitude	Elevation Gain	Difficulty
0	8,500 ft	0	none

Map: 52. Continuing past the Alluvial Fan (No. 68) another mile or two, you will reach the end of the paved road at a fork whose right branch is the famous "Old Fall River Road" (one-way to the visitor center at Fall River Pass), and whose left branch meanders into the Endovalley picnic area. This is an enchanting loop that passes by numerous lunch spots (many of them along a placid stretch of the Fall River). Mid-afternoon on a weekday is probably the best time to arrive if you want a picnic table. Of course that means we are suggesting an evening meal rather than lunch. Go for it. Hamburgers will never taste better than here.

LECTOR: The title of this book says "lunch spots."

AUCTOR: I see you are a legalistic type. One supper among 100+ lunches is not unreasonable.

LECTOR: What if everybody bends the truth when it seems convenient?

AUCTOR: I take it we must act only on that maxim which should become a universal law?

LECTOR: Kant said it better.

AUCTOR: There are better moral theologians, too.

70 CHASM FALLS

Distance	Altitude	Elevation Gain	Difficulty
0.1 miles (round trip)	9,000 ft	NA	trivial

Map: 52. This impressive torrent is about two miles up the one-way Fall River Road, not far above Horseshoe Park. The asphalt path that runs down from the parking area is steep and sometimes slippery with moisture or gravel. Tourists in street shoes travel it at their risk. But it's short, and the view of the falls is worth a picture. If you don't mind having lunch near a constant flow of people, this is a good spot. We do not advise (as we have elsewhere) moving off into the woods to a more private place. Crossing the Fall River here is dangerous.

71 MOUNT CHAPIN

Distance	Altitude	Elevation Gain	Difficulty
1.5 miles	12,454 ft	1,800 ft	moderate

Map: 52. Now that you are on the one-way part of Old Fall River Road (No. 70), there is nothing for it but to continue upward. Near timberline you will come to a small parking space below Chapin Pass. Because this trailhead is so high (10,600+ ft) compared to most others, the hikes that start here are relatively easy. Recently our daughter Joan and her husband (both desk-bound in Wisconsin) and their five-year-old twins went up Mt. Chapin with me (close to 70 at the time), with no complaints from anyone in the party. We recommend it as a good introduction to high-altitude hiking.

Drive to the trailhead early to get a parking space. Climb the steps to the pass and leave the Chapin Creek trail (which continues north, downhill) on a path that heads east toward Mt. Chapin. In less than a mile of sometimes steep hiking you will be contouring along the west flank of Chapin. If you stay on this trail (which grows fainter) too long, you will contour around the peak—somewhere you need to head up and climb to the top. You will probably reach a false summit first, but the true top is not far beyond. There are interesting gullies along the way (often filled with snow), plunging down the precipitous south side of Chapin. Look, but do not get too close. Enjoy lunch on the top.

72 MOUNT CHIQUITA

Distance	Altitude	Elevation Gain	Difficulty
2.5 miles	13,069 ft	2,400 ft	moderate

Map: 52. This easy thirteener may be climbed from Mt. Chapin (No. 71) by going down to the pass between the two peaks and then up. The loss of altitude is irritating, but the view (with lunch) compensates.

LECTOR: How many times do you eat lunch in one day?

AUCTOR: There are several schools of thought on this subject. Some folks eat off and on all day (thus justifying our listing of consecutive lunch spots on a single hike). Others prefer to wait until the highest point is reached (because digestion requires blood that might be feeding the brain, resulting in dizziness or worse if you are still climbing). Still others postpone lunch until they are well on the way back to the car, perhaps feeling insecure too far into the wild. A few (especially those who wait so long that they are soaked by an afternoon storm) never eat lunch at all. They are to be more pitied than censured, for they will have missed the whole point of hiking in the Park.

LECTOR: Are you a college professor?

AUCTOR: Why do you ask?

LECTOR: You have a tendency to lecture.

AUCTOR: I take that to be a compliment.

73 YPSILON MOUNTAIN

Distance	Altitude	Elevation Gain	Difficulty
3.5 miles	13,514 ft	2,900 ft	hard

Maps: 52, 76. Climbing Ypsilon from Chiquita (No. 72) is much like doing Chiquita from Chapin, except the loss of altitude is greater and the top is farther off. Never mind—it's not very hard, just tiring. Snow-filled gullies along the way (as on Mt. Chapin) are worthy of note, and the view from the top, down the east face to Spectacle Lakes (No. 62, page 55), is dizzying. We have often used these peaks (Chapin, Chiquita, and Ypsilon) as conditioning for Longs Peak (which is 741 feet higher than Ypsilon). It's a good idea to have at least one thirteener under your belt before doing Longs.

FALL RIVER ROAD TRAILHEADS 69

Now you have climbed all the major peaks of the Mummy Range (Chapin, Chiquita, Ypsilon, Fairchild, Hagues, and Mummy).

LECTOR: Are you under the impression that I am visiting all your lunch spots?

AUCTOR: Why not?

LECTOR: I'm only here for two weeks, and I rest for a day between hikes.

74 THE WHALE

Distance	Altitude	Elevation Gain	Difficulty
8 miles (round trip)	11,500 ft	900 ft	hard

Map: 52. One of our favorite hikes takes off from the Mt. Chapin trail (No. 71) as it contours along the slope of Chapin. Head down a short distance (northeast) into the valley below Chiquita and Ypsilon, then climb back up to tree line on the western slope of Chiquita (or Ypsilon, depending on where you left the Chapin trail). We usually make a game of counting the deer and elk along the way, never failing to see at least 25.

LECTOR: The hills are alive.

AUCTOR: With the sound of bugling.

Contouring north along the slope, you will step over several brooks draining the peaks above, and will probably see mysterious circles of churned-up mud as you pass below Ypsilon. We think these are evidence of bears, but maybe not—perhaps they are due to aliens. Eventually you will come to a real stream, running down west through the trees to join Chapin Creek far below. On the other side of the stream looms a large bulwark of a hill (running up to the ridge joining Ypsilon and Desolation Peaks) that we think looks like a whale (and have so christened it). Giving thanks for lunch at this point seems like the thing to do. The whole hike has been a wilderness experience (as they say)—not a fellow human to be seen anywhere.

The experience deepens (unless you choose to return the way you came). We like to go down the stream (which requires some bushwhacking and occasional crossings) all the way to Chapin Creek. This involves a considerable loss of altitude, because you have to climb back out of the valley (south) to reach Chapin Pass (where you started early in the morning). A trail appears on the west side of Chapin Creek as you go uphill (often through swampy terrain)—the first sign of civilization after a day in the wild.

If you don't agree with us that this lunch trip is one of the best in the Park, we recommend that you drive on up the road to the store at Fall River Pass and have a hamburger.

75 DESOLATION PEAKS

Distance	Altitude	Elevation Gain	Difficulty
5.5 miles	12,949 ft	2,300 ft	hard

Map: 52. Perhaps the Whale (No. 74) whetted your appetite for more wilderness. In that case, cross the stream and continue north, up the hill and through the trees, leveling out to contour around the base of the Whale. There is a sort of pass through a rocky gap that will bring you past the Whale, to the slope that heads east up the ridge between Ypsilon and Desolation Peaks. (The plural refers to the several high points along the ridge.) We have seen herds of bighorn sheep on this slope, a rare treat indeed.

After climbing to the top of the ridge (where you can peer into the void on the other side), you have a choice. The prudent decision is to go back down. If you decide to head out to the highest of the Desolation Peaks, be careful. The scramble along the ridge to the top is exposed in places, and it's a long way down. The summit rocks leave barely adequate room for lunch. But it's worth the effort. Use extra caution on the way back—accidents are most likely when hikers are tired.

It is worth mentioning that climbing Desolation Peaks by this route (below Ypsilon, around the Whale, and then up) avoids a harder scramble along the ridge from the top of Ypsilon (and of course does not require climbing Ypsilon). We recommend it as a preferable alternative to the standard route.

Boulder Bruchetta Picnic
Suzanne and Brian Kauffman, Colorado

You'll need:

1 unsliced loaf of fresh baked bread
4 oz extra virgin olive oil
2-3 tomatoes, ideally vine ripened
2-3 balls of fresh mozzarella cheese
8-10 fresh basil leaves
Yields about 4-6 open faced sandwiches.

Slice the bread to 1/2 inch thick,
drizzle 1-2 tablespoons of olive oil over the top,
next place a layer of sliced mozzarella cheese
followed by a layer of tomato slices.
Finally, top with 2-3 basil leaves.

Complete this meal with fruit salad, pasta salad, and a bottle of wine.

While you can find all these ingredients in many towns, if you happen to be passing through Boulder on your way to "the Park", you can get all that you need there and experience a quick insider's view of Boulder in the process. On Broadway in Boulder, just a few blocks north of the popular Pearl Street Mall, you can find excellent, fresh baked bread at the Breadworks Bakery (2644 Broadway). Just across the street to the north is the Ideal Market (1275 Alpine Dr), a local favorite. Here you'll find fresh mozzarella cheese, tomatoes, basil, and all the other fixin's, including delicious deli salads. Between these two stores is the Boulder Wine Merchant with a nice selection of wines. Finally, right next door to the Wine Merchant is Vic's Coffee Shop where you can grab a latte' for the road. Now just head north out of town and you'll reach RMNP in about an hour. Have fun!

72 A HIKING GUIDE TO RMNP

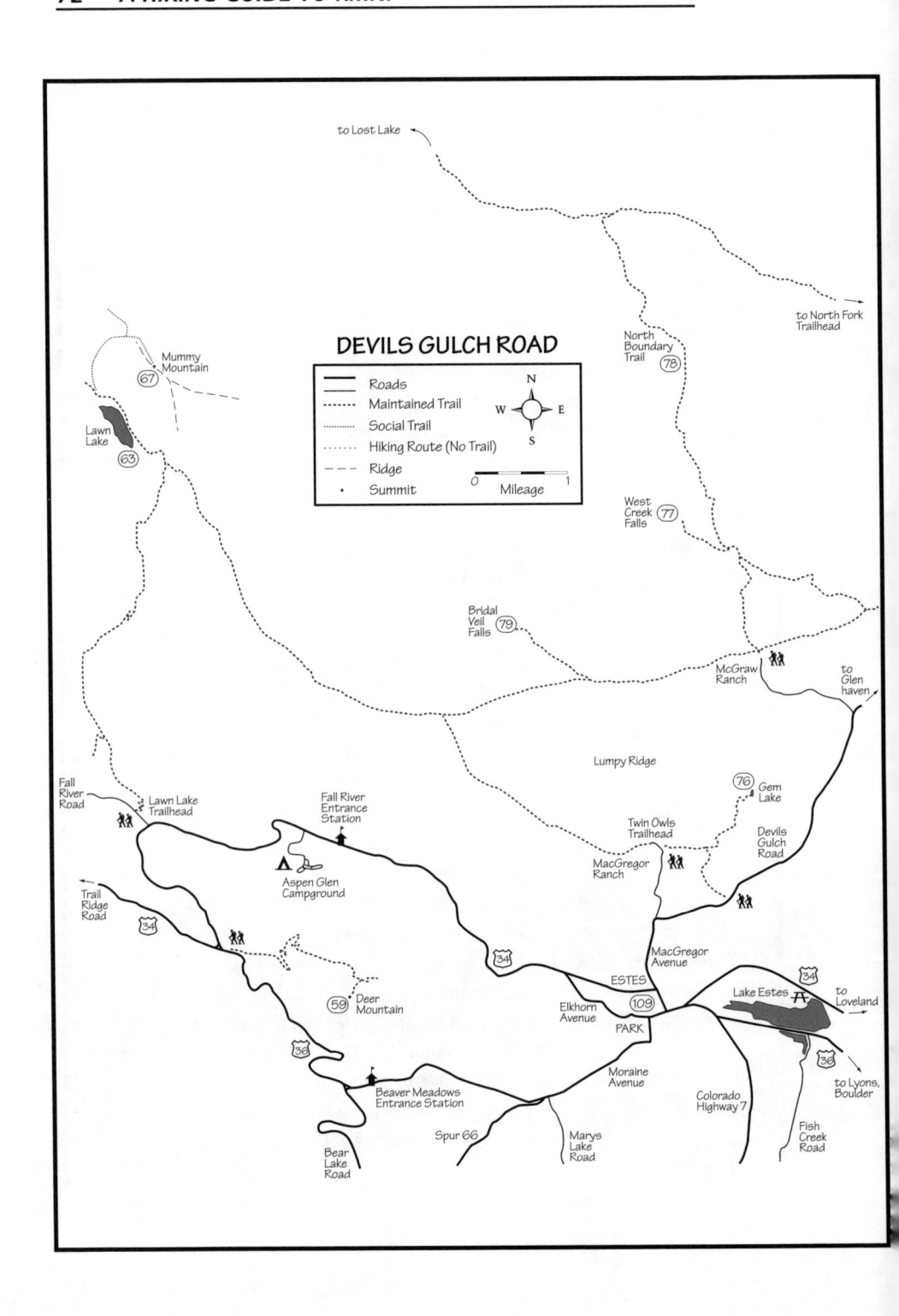

DEVILS GULCH ROAD TRAILHEADS

76 GEM LAKE

Distance	Altitude	Elevation Gain	Difficulty
2 miles	8,800 ft	900 ft	easy

Maps: 72, 76. Drive north out of Estes Park on the US 34 bypass, which immediately turns west to an intersection with MacGregor Avenue (later called Devils Gulch Road). Turn right (north) until you come to MacGregor Ranch about a mile from town. Instead of turning east on the main road, continue north into the ranch to the Twin Owls parking lot. The trail to Gem Lake starts here, rising for almost two miles to the lake. The cliffs along the shore are unusual, as is the lake itself—disappointing to some hikers, but in fact a nice place to have lunch. Not every lake in the Park must be alpine: this one may remind you of Arkansas.

Another trail to Gem Lake starts a mile further east, at a parking lot off Devils Gulch Road. It is slightly longer, and the altitude gain is larger (but not much).

As we go to press, there is talk of replacing these trailheads with a new one, still off Devils Gulch Road. Signs will provide directions.

77 WEST CREEK FALLS

Distance	Altitude	Elevation Gain	Difficulty
8 miles	8,200 ft	600 ft (twice)	moderate

Maps: 72, 76. About two miles beyond the MacGregor Ranch entrance on Devils Gulch Road (see No. 76), there is an unpaved road that turns off northeast and then goes west and north to the old McGraw Ranch—now a part of the Park. Signs inform you that it is a private road—no trespassing. But it provides the only public access (by car) to a Park trailhead, which means that the signs are obsolete. Nobody should challenge you on the way to the ranch. Parking is available at the end of the road, along its edge.

Hike west from the trailhead for a short distance to the North Boundary trail, which climbs north over a 600-ft ridge and then descends even more to a bridge that crosses West Creek. A little farther up the trail a spur runs off northwest to West Creek Falls, as pretty a spot for lunch as you could wish.

The return trip requires climbing up the ridge again, which depresses some people. There is a longer alternate route, down an unimproved trail that follows West Creek (on its north side) toward Glen Haven. Eventually it meets Cow Creek coming in from McGraw Ranch (where you started). Unfortunately there are no bridges here—you have to wade across West Creek, or risk your well-being on a log. The wading is no problem, but it delays progress, since you will need to dry your feet and put your boots back on (unless you waded in your boots). You are not in a hurry on these hikes, are you?

On the east side of Cow Creek there is a rudimentary path that goes up the creek, crossing it again on a road that returns to the trailhead at McGraw Ranch. The road appears to be in the National Forest on its way back into the Park, but it passes by a private residence and pond—do not trespass. Back at the ranch you may wonder whether this alternate route was worth it. The work done is certainly greater than the effort climbing the ridge. On the other hand, it is prettier.

78 NORTH BOUNDARY TRAIL

Distance	Altitude	Elevation Gain	Difficulty
5.5 miles	8,900 ft	1,300 ft	moderate

Maps: 72, 76. If you were depressed by climbing over a ridge and back on the West Creek Falls hike (No. 77), you may be well advised to skip this one. For it involves *three* ridges (over and back). On the other hand, there are several lovely streams to cross, each offering a pleasant lunch spot. The hike is also a balm to those who are tired of having to get somewhere. The North Boundary trail (which follows the *east* boundary of the Park) starts at the McGraw Ranch (see No. 77) and ends at the North Fork trail (see No. 80). Except for a ranger cabin shortly before the end, there is no compelling reason to keep going—you can turn around anywhere without feeling that you didn't succeed.

On a hike back from Lost Lake (No. 80) we stopped at the ranger cabin in a heavy rain, and lo! there was a ranger inside who offered us hot coffee. Even more remarkable, he was from Harvard, and a book lay open upon a table—*A Theory of Justice,* by the Harvard philosophy professor John Rawls. My wife had been reading the book at the time, which naturally led to some conversation with the ranger. Thus does the Park Service cater to the needs of backcountry hikers.

79 BRIDAL VEIL FALLS

Distance	Altitude	Elevation Gain	Difficulty
3 miles	8,900 ft	1,300 ft	moderate

Maps: 72, 76. Starting at McGraw Ranch (see No. 77), follow the ranch road and Cow Creek trail west and northwest to the falls. The gradient is mostly gentle and there are lovely lunch spots at the falls.

80 LOST LAKE

Distance	Altitude	Elevation Gain	Difficulty
9.5 miles	10,700 ft	2,800 ft	hard

Map: 76. Drive down Devils Gulch Road (see No. 76) through Glen Haven, continuing about two miles beyond the village to the entrance of the Retreat. Turn left across the North Fork of the Big Thompson and drive to the end of the road (ignoring turn-offs). Park at the Dunraven Glade trailhead and start what is the longest hike we ever did in one day. The trail goes uphill for a short distance, then down to follow the North Fork (mostly west) for many miles to Lost Lake. Despite the name, Trail's End Cheley Camp (about a mile from the start) is not the end of the trail—the hike continues past Deserted Village, past the ranger cabin on the North Boundary trail (No. 78), past Aspen Meadow to a fork (take the left branch), past Lost Falls and Lost Meadow, past Las Vegas, and finally reaches Lost Lake. You can stop almost anywhere and find a pleasant lunch spot. Lost Falls is shown on maps near the fork (where the Stormy Peaks trail branches off to the northwest), but we didn't find it.

LECTOR: Of course not. It's lost. I'm surprised you found the lake.

AUCTOR: I wish you had been with us on this hike. You help to pass the time.

81 LAKE HUSTED

Distance	Altitude	Elevation Gain	Difficulty
10 miles	11,100 ft	3,100 ft	hard

Map: 76. Lost Lake (No. 80) is at the end of the trail, but it is easy to go on. Half a mile west, up a gentle tundra slope, lies Lake Husted, where lunch can be restorative after the long hike in.

76 A HIKING GUIDE TO RMNP

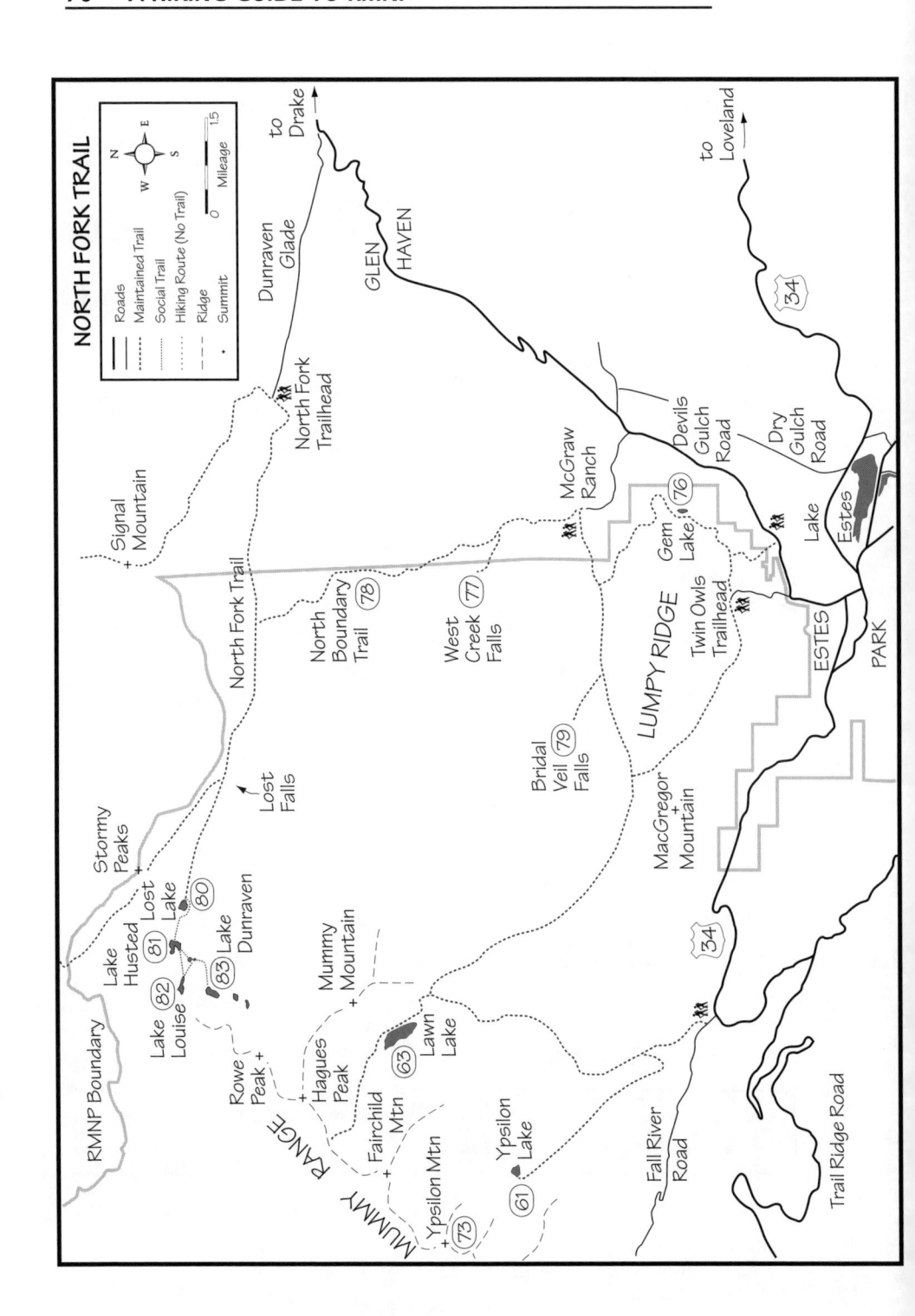

82 LAKE LOUISE

Distance	Altitude	Elevation Gain	Difficulty
10.5 miles	11,000 ft	3,100 ft	hard

Maps: 52, 76. This is another half-mile west from Lake Husted (No. 81), a little downhill. Can we say with a straight face that you ought to have lunch here, too?

> LECTOR: I have learned to pack multiple lunches, one for each place you invite me to visit. My pack weighs twenty pounds and my girth is increasing, but when I get back home I'll start exercising.
>
> AUCTOR: Angels and ministers of grace, defend us.
>
> LECTOR: I thought we weren't going to quote Hamlet.

83 LAKE DUNRAVEN

Distance	Altitude	Elevation Gain	Difficulty
11 miles	11,300 ft	3,300 ft	hard

Maps: 52, 76. From Lake Husted or Lake Louise (No. 81 and 82) you can find the North Fork again by heading southwest or southeast, respectively, to a couple of unnamed lakes below Lake Dunraven. Climb up south on the ridge from the lower of these, until you can see the way west to Lake Dunraven. Have some more lunch—it's a long way back.

78 A HIKING GUIDE TO RMNP

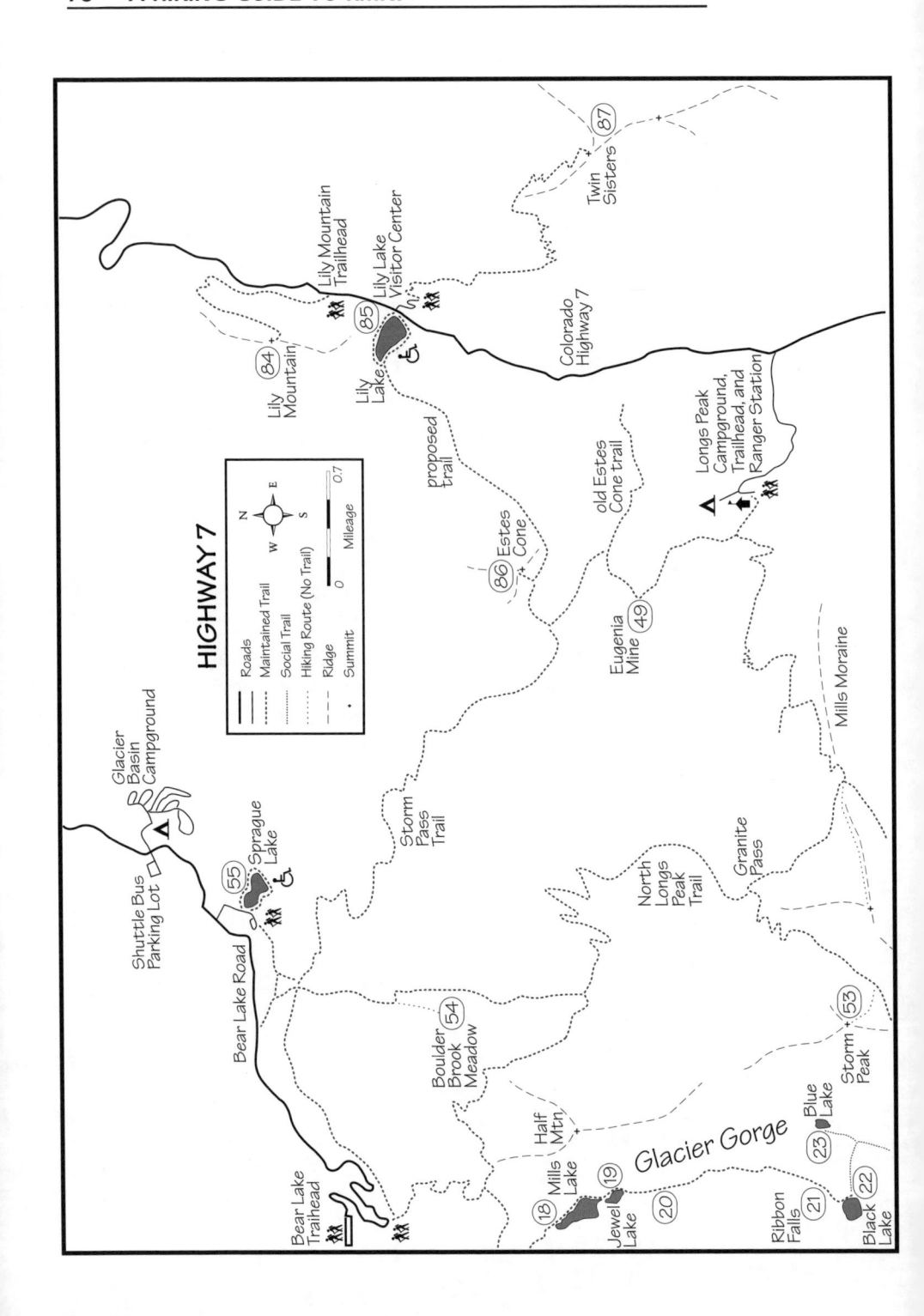

COLORADO HIGHWAY 7 TRAILHEADS

84 LILY MOUNTAIN

Distance	Altitude	Elevation Gain	Difficulty
2 miles	9,786 ft	1,000 ft	moderate

Map: 78. Drive up Colorado 7 about six miles to the Lily Mountain trailhead on the west side of the road (easy to miss and short on parking space). The trail goes north longer than it seems it should, then switchbacks through the trees (often indistinctly) to the rocks at the summit. These rocks require some clambering, surprising on such a modest mountain (really a foothill). The rewarding view from the top includes the Longs Peak cirque; reason enough to be here for lunch.

85 LILY LAKE CIRCUIT

Distance	Altitude	Elevation Gain	Difficulty
0.5 miles	8,900 ft	0	trivial

Map: 78. The Park Service has opened another visitor center here (about 6½ miles up Colorado 7 from Estes Park). There is also an improved trail around the lake. Have lunch almost anywhere along the tranquil shore.

86 ESTES CONE

Distance	Altitude	Elevation Gain	Difficulty
3 miles	11,006 ft	1,600 ft	moderate

Map: 78. This mountain (barely qualifying for the name) used to be approached from the Storm Pass trailhead, which was hard to find, poorly marked, and short on parking space. A few years ago local property owners withdrew permission for any parking at all. This raised the question of public access, unhappily resolved by various authorities suggesting that hikers should walk in from Colorado 7 (which adds almost two miles to the round trip), or hike from the Longs Peak trailhead (starting higher, but adding three miles to the round trip and more congestion at the already crowded Longs Peak parking lot).

The Park Service is responding to this unreasonable state of affairs by constructing a new trail up Estes Cone, starting at Lily Lake (No. 85). We have not hiked it yet, but it promises to be at least as good as the old one. For the present, we recommend starting at the Longs Peak trailhead (if you can find a place to park). Hike past Eugenia Mine and Moore Park (see No. 49, page 45) to the junction with the old Storm Pass trail. Follow it up to Storm Pass, where an unimproved trail turns right to head up the last part of the "cone". Some scrambling over rocks is required at the end, providing the right amount of stress for enjoyment of lunch at the top. The view of the Longs Peak cirque is superb—in fact no direction will disappoint. It is our favorite mountain for introduction of friends to climbing.

87 TWIN SISTERS

Distance	Altitude	Elevation Gain	Difficulty
4 miles	11,428 ft	2,500 ft	moderate

Map: 78. There is a new trail up this mountain, too. Park at the Lily Lake visitor center (see No. 85) and hike up the numerous switchbacks to the pass between the Crags (on the north) and the top. The rest of the trail is above timberline, exposed to dangerous lightning strikes when a storm moves in (as it often does). The view across Tahosa Valley to Longs Peak is impressive. We often do this hike in the evening, timing things so that we still have light until we are back in the trees on the way down. After that, moonlight (or a flashlight) is adequate. Of course that changes the top to a supper spot, but it avoids the afternoon storms. It used to be popular to hike up Twin Sisters to watch the sunrise from the top, which then became a breakfast spot.

> LECTOR: There must be a commandment forbidding breakfast at the top of a mountain.
>
> AUCTOR: Moses must have gotten awfully hungry.

COLORADO HIGHWAY 7 TRAILHEADS 81

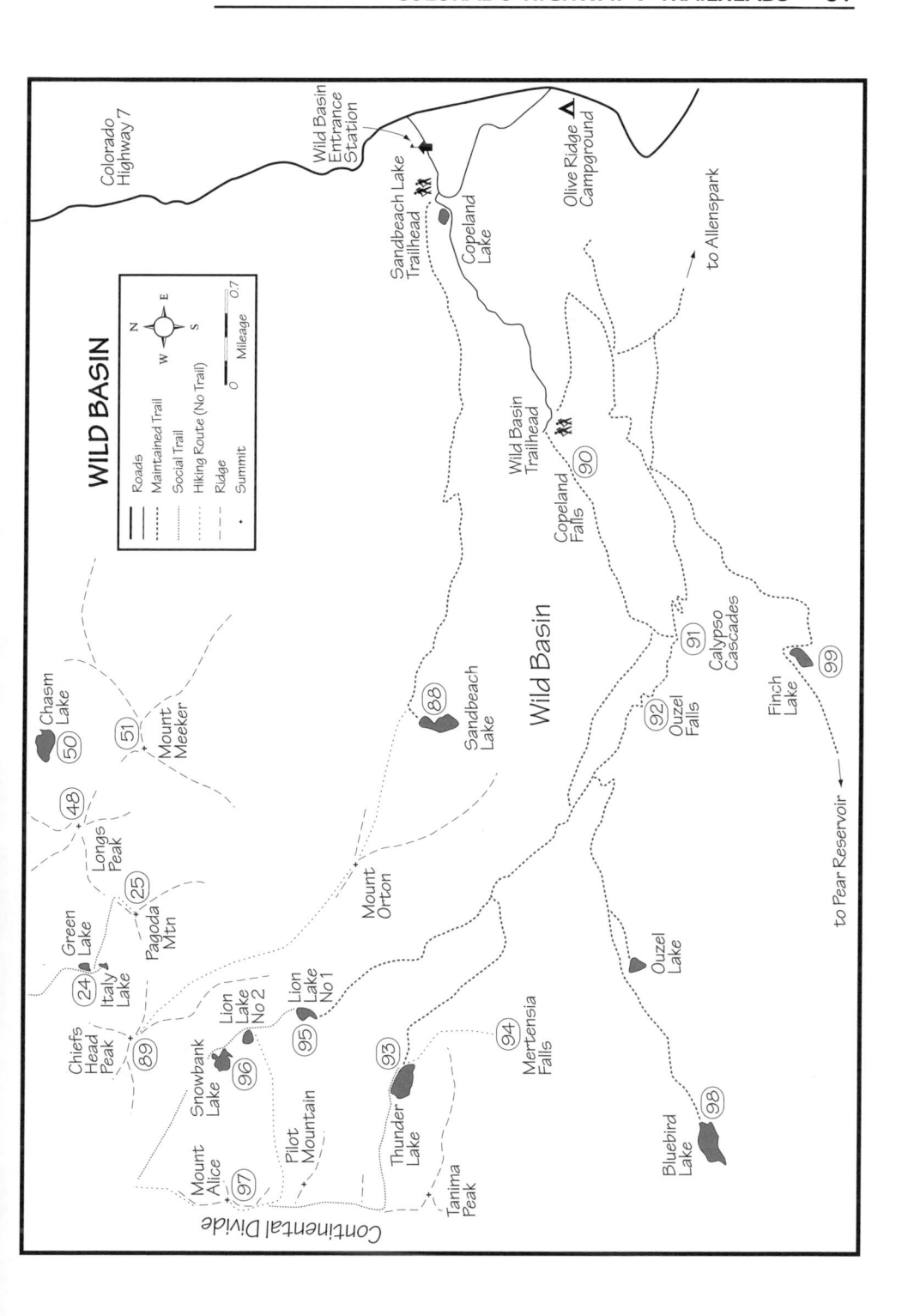

WILD BASIN TRAILS

88 SANDBEACH LAKE

Distance	Altitude	Elevation Gain	Difficulty
4 miles	10,300 ft	2,000 ft	moderate

Map: 81. Almost thirteen miles from Estes Park on Colorado 7, turn right (west) on the road to Wild Basin. The Sandbeach Lake trailhead is a short distance farther, on the right. Follow the trail (mostly west) to the lake, noting the stream crossings along the way (possible lunch spots if you decide to stop before reaching the lake, or on the return trip). The lake itself is surrounded by a sandy shoreline (visible from the top of Longs Peak)—which explains its name.

89 CHIEFS HEAD PEAK

Distance	Altitude	Elevation Gain	Difficulty
7 miles	13,579 ft	5,300 ft	hard

Map: 78. If you are interested in climbing Chiefs Head (third highest in the Park, at the end of Glacier Gorge, but hard to climb from there), you can take off from the Sandbeach Lake trail (No. 88), at the point where it begins its descent to the lake. Work your way northwest through the trees, then up the ridge toward Mt. Orton (little better than a rocky knob on your left). From there it is a straight shot up the North Ridge to the top of Chiefs Head. More precisely, it's a long haul; the elevation gain of this hike is the greatest of any in this book. But the view down into Glacier Gorge, and around the panorama of peaks that present themselves in all directions, is magnificent.

90 COPELAND FALLS

Distance	Altitude	Elevation Gain	Difficulty
0.25 miles	8,500 ft	15 ft	easy

Map: 81. Follow the Wild Basin Road (see No. 88) to the ranger station and parking lot, about two miles from the Park entrance near Copeland Lake. Some parts of the road are not made for vehicles to pass in opposite directions—if you meet somebody, one party may have to pull over, or even back up to a wider space. Nor is a parking space guaranteed. The cure for all this (as elsewhere) is to arrive early.

Copeland Falls (only a quarter-mile from the trailhead) is not very high, but the volume of water pouring over it at high velocity seems greater than the capacity of the river itself.

LECTOR: That's a paradox.

AUCTOR: No worse than the stars that the cosmologists claim are older than the universe.

LECTOR: Do you believe that?

AUCTOR: Certainly not. But I believe they'll get it right.

91 CALYPSO CASCADES

Distance	Altitude	Elevation Gain	Difficulty
2 miles	9,200 ft	700 ft	moderate

Map: 81. Start at the Wild Basin ranger station (see No. 90) and follow the North St. Vrain Trail past Copeland Falls to a bridge that crosses the river. The trail soon leaves the St. Vrain to climb up along Cony Creek to Calypso Cascades, an unusual network of multiple waterfalls that is very scenic. When you get there, don't turn left—that will take you back east toward Allenspark. Cross the bridges over the stream and melt into the woods for an enchanted lunch (or keep going—there are wonderful places ahead).

LECTOR: Define "enchanted lunch."

AUCTOR: Sandwich of your choice, potato sticks, fresh fruit, candy bar and soft drink (both at the temperature of the stream); musical water falling down moss-covered rocks; dappled sunshine; deep blue sky; soft, level, grassy or pine-needled seating backed by a tree or rock; wildflowers; quaking aspen and ponderosa pine; 75° with gentle breeze; congenial companions; no agenda.

LECTOR: How many places like that have you been?

AUCTOR: At least fifty. What did you think this book was about?

92 OUZEL FALLS

Distance	Altitude	Elevation Gain	Difficulty
3 miles	9,500 ft	1,000 ft	moderate

Map: 81. This popular waterfall, a mile up the trail from Calypso Cascades (No. 91), is high enough to hurt people who get too close—one lad who tried to jump across the stream at the top was killed. The best place to be is at the bottom, a respectful distance away, perhaps on a large boulder next to the stream. You have to leave the main trail (just before the bridge) and scramble a few yards to get there, but it isn't far, just moist. If you want to peer down the falls, there is a way up (a few yards past the bridge, on the left), but it requires care. Numerous spots for lunch will present themselves—stay away from the edges!

93 THUNDER LAKE

Distance	Altitude	Elevation Gain	Difficulty
7 miles	10,600 ft	2,100 ft	hard

Map: 81. Start at the Wild Basin ranger station and follow the North St. Vrain trail past Calypso Cascades (No. 91) and Ouzel Falls (No. 92). If Thunder Lake is your principal objective, you need not visit these spots at all, though you'll miss some beautiful scenery. About a mile from the trailhead, shortly before the bridge that crosses the St. Vrain River, a sign points to some campgrounds up an unimproved trail that branches off to the right. This path cuts off a loop of the freeway, rejoining it beyond Ouzel Falls. The rest of the hike to the lake is long, gently uphill, and pleasant. Along the way you can see Mertensia Falls across the St. Vrain valley (No. 94).

There is a small ranger cabin at Thunder Lake, surrounded by stunning scenery. The sheer east face of Mt. Alice (No. 97) looms over the valley to the northwest, with other peaks of the Continental Divide marching south toward the boundary of the Park. Boulder-Grand Pass (west of the lake) lures the backpacker over the Divide and down a chain of lakes to the East Inlet trail that ends at Grand Lake. Since you are presumably not backpacking, enjoy a well-earned lunch in the meadow below the cabin.

94 MERTENSIA FALLS

Distance	Altitude	Elevation Gain	Difficulty
8 miles	10,400 ft	1900 ft	hard

Map: 81. When you first see this waterfall, from a point about 5.5 miles up the Thunder Lake trail (No. 93), you may be inclined to descend into the valley and climb back up again to the falls. Too much bushwhacking, and a less than secure crossing of the St. Vrain River, argue against it. The easy (but longer) way is to go to Thunder Lake first, and then walk down through the open woods on the other side of the stream. Of course this takes time (and you will want to go back the same way)—we did it on a magical two-day tour made possible by the rangers in our family, who got permission for us to sleep overnight in the cabin at Thunder Lake.

LECTOR: Why are you telling me this?

AUCTOR: I admit to a certain selfish satisfaction.

LECTOR: I'd call it a certain perverse pride.

AUCTOR: That doesn't alliterate as well.

95 LION LAKES

Distance	Altitude	Elevation Gain	Difficulty
7.5 miles	11,400 ft	2,900 ft	hard

Map: 81. Coming up the Thunder Lake trail (No. 93), you may have noticed a branch going off to the right (about five miles from the trailhead). It's easy to miss with your head down, but there is a sign directing you to Lion Lakes. The first of these is two miles up the branch, in a meadow that is conducive to lunch. But there are great things ahead. First comes the famous Trio Falls.

LECTOR: Why "famous"?

AUCTOR: In our family, anyway. In the summer of 1961, engaged to the girl who became the mother of our children, I invited her to go up Mt. Alice (her first mountain). Resting at Trio Falls, I brought out a small flask of Kentucky sour mash bourbon, mixing it with water from the stream and offering it as a celebration of our progress (both romantic and alpine).

LECTOR: You know, I may have the wrong impression of you.

AUCTOR: The thing is, my wife denies that it happened.

LECTOR: Well, did it?

AUCTOR: It was a long time ago.

LECTOR: Like General Pershing, if you didn't do it, you should have.

AUCTOR: Your short-term memory is fine. General Pershing was back at Dream Lake (No. 3).

Not far above Trio Falls you'll find Lion Lake No. 2 (above tree-line), and then Snowbank Lake (No. 96). Each is a tempting lunch spot, especially if you originally intended to climb Mt. Alice (No. 97) and are now pooping out.

LECTOR: I'm going strong.

AUCTOR: Did I tell you that Mt. Alice is an eighteen-mile round trip?

LECTOR: We haven't got to No. 97 yet.

96 SNOWBANK LAKE

Distance	Altitude	Elevation Gain	Difficulty
8 miles	11,500 ft	3,000 ft	hard

Map: 81. This lake is less than a half-mile above Lion Lake No. 2 (see No. 95). It is easy to give up here and turn around. On the other hand, having come so far and climbed so high, it's a shame to stop. You are less than 2000 feet below the summit of Mt. Alice (No. 97), with only a mile to go. Save the rest of your lunch and soldier on.

97 MOUNT ALICE

Distance	Altitude	Elevation Gain	Difficulty
9 miles	13,310 ft	4,800 ft	hard

Map: 81. From Snowbank Lake (No. 96) it's a piece of cake. Simply trudge up the endless slope to the pass between Alice and Chiefs Head, turn left to cross a hairy-looking neck (Hourglass Ridge) leading to Alice, and climb up the forbidding summit slope to the top. Nothing to it. Be sure to study the fabulous east face of Alice on the way up, and the backsides of McHenrys, Chiefs Head, Pagoda, Longs, and Meeker.

You still have to get down. Dooie and I descended between Alice and Pilot Mountain, but the usual route follows the Continental Divide to Boulder-Grand Pass and then down to Thunder Lake.

LECTOR: Who's Dooie?

AUCTOR: The girl I married—her real name is Cordelia.

LECTOR: That's a nice name.

AUCTOR: King Lear liked it.

98   BLUEBIRD LAKE

Distance	Altitude	Elevation Gain	Difficulty
6 miles	11,000 ft	2,500 ft	hard

Map: 81. Back at Ouzel Falls (No. 92, page 84) it is about half a mile farther up the St. Vrain trail to a fork whose right branch is the Thunder Lake trail and whose left branch goes to Bluebird Lake. Apart from its intrinsic beauty, the route is chiefly interesting because of the 1978 fire that scorched much of it, and because of the Bluebird Lake dam that the Park Service acquired (from Longmont) and removed—to prevent another disaster like the 1982 Lawn Lake flood. The dam was so skillfully broken up and carried out (mostly by helicopter) that it is difficult today to see where it was (although my wife and I once saw a shovel that was inadvertently left behind). A nice place for lunch.

99   FINCH LAKE

Distance	Altitude	Elevation Gain	Difficulty
5 miles	9,900 ft	1,400 ft	moderate

Map: 81. The Finch Lake trailhead is on the south side of the Wild Basin Road, a short distance before the ranger station. The trail climbs eastward for about a mile, then switches back to the west through lovely meadows and aspen groves. A junction with the trail to Allenspark comes up in about half a mile—keep going west for another mile to an intersection where one trail goes west to Calypso Cascades (see No. 91, page 83) and east to Allenspark. Stay on the Finch Lake trail (southwest) as it climbs into the Ouzel burn area and out again, finally descending to the lake through beautiful woods. The peaks encircling the lake are wonderful to behold. The best place for lunch is a short way around the northeastern shoreline to a charming inlet where you can cool your supply of liquids.

88   A HIKING GUIDE TO RMNP

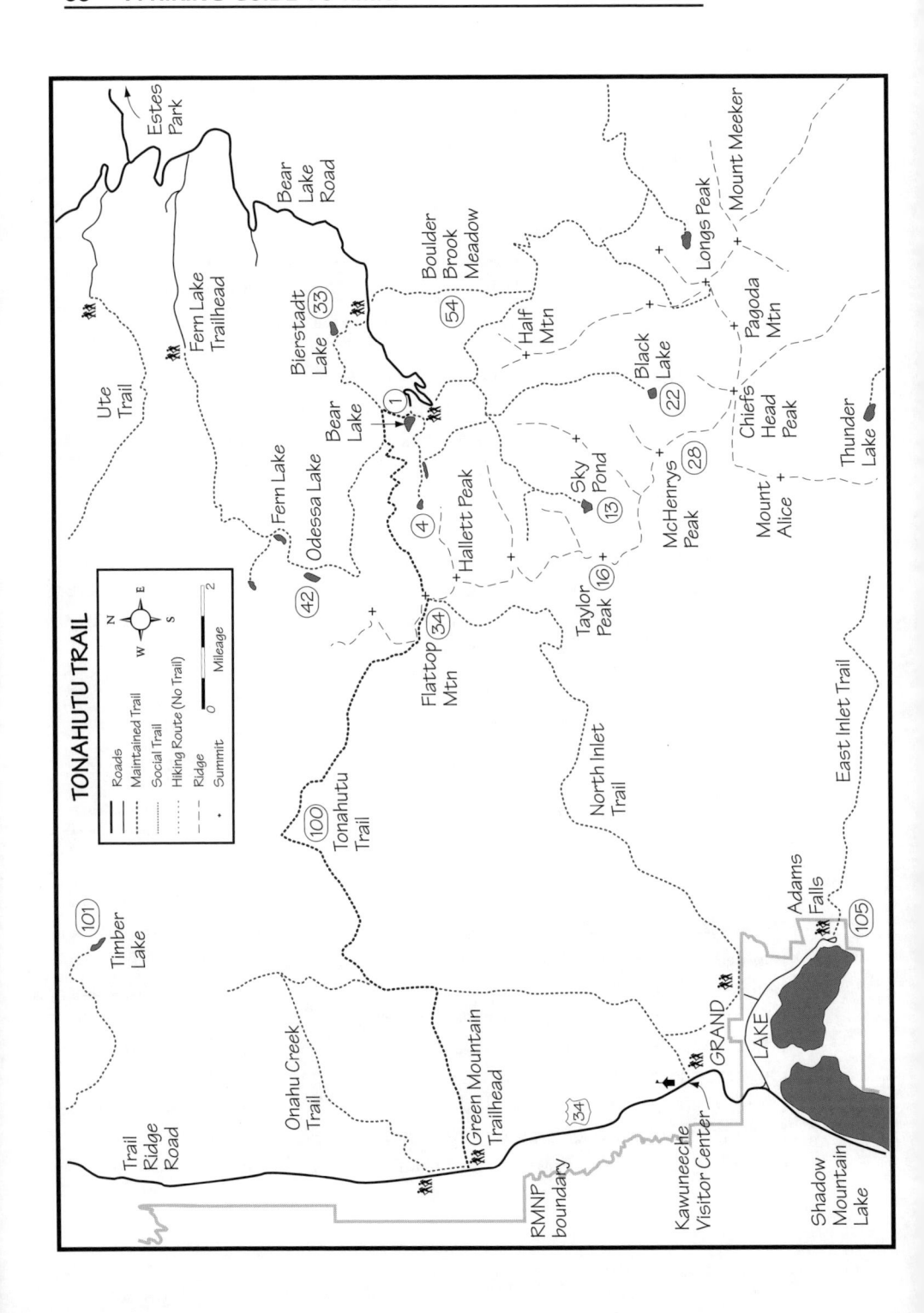

WEST SIDE TRAILS

100 THE TONAHUTU TRAIL

Distance	Altitude	Elevation Gain	Difficulty
15 miles	12,324 ft	2,800 ft	hard

Maps: 8, 34, 88. Find someone willing to pick you up at the Green Mountain trailhead on Trail Ridge Road, west of the Continental Divide, or leave a car there yourself. Then, starting at Bear Lake, follow the Flattop trail (No. 34, page 33) for 4.5 miles to the point near the top where the trail divides (marked by two large cairns). The left branch is the North Inlet trail—beautiful but long (going all the way to Grand Lake). We have usually backpacked on this trail, spending a night at one of the campsites along the way. Since this book is about lunch spots, not backpacking expeditions, we will say no more (though there are wonderful mountains and lakes that are accessible from the North Inlet trail).

The Tonahutu trail takes off to the right (west) from the Flattop cairns, following the Continental Divide as far as Notchtop (see No. 37, page 35 and No. 42, page 38). Then it runs northwest across the Bighorn Flats, gradually descending the western slope to tree line, where it turns south and west and south again to follow Tonahutu Creek. One good place for lunch is Granite Falls, but there are many others along the way. Stop when you get hungry. Rather than hiking all the way to Grand Lake, turn off at the Green Mountain trail (after some 10 miles downhill), descending west for another half-mile to the parking lot on Trail Ridge Road. There you will see the friendly person who agreed to pick you up, or the car you left the day before (if you got a permit for overnight parking). You will feel the fifteen miles you have put between you and Bear Lake (not as the crow flies, but as the human hikes). It is a good feeling.

LECTOR: Speak for yourself.

AUCTOR: Did you not like the hike?

LECTOR: Somewhere along Big Meadows my feet began to hurt. I had no band-aids, no lunch left, no poncho, and it began to rain.

AUCTOR: Didn't I tell you to pack a poncho?

LECTOR: No.

90 A HIKING GUIDE TO RMNP

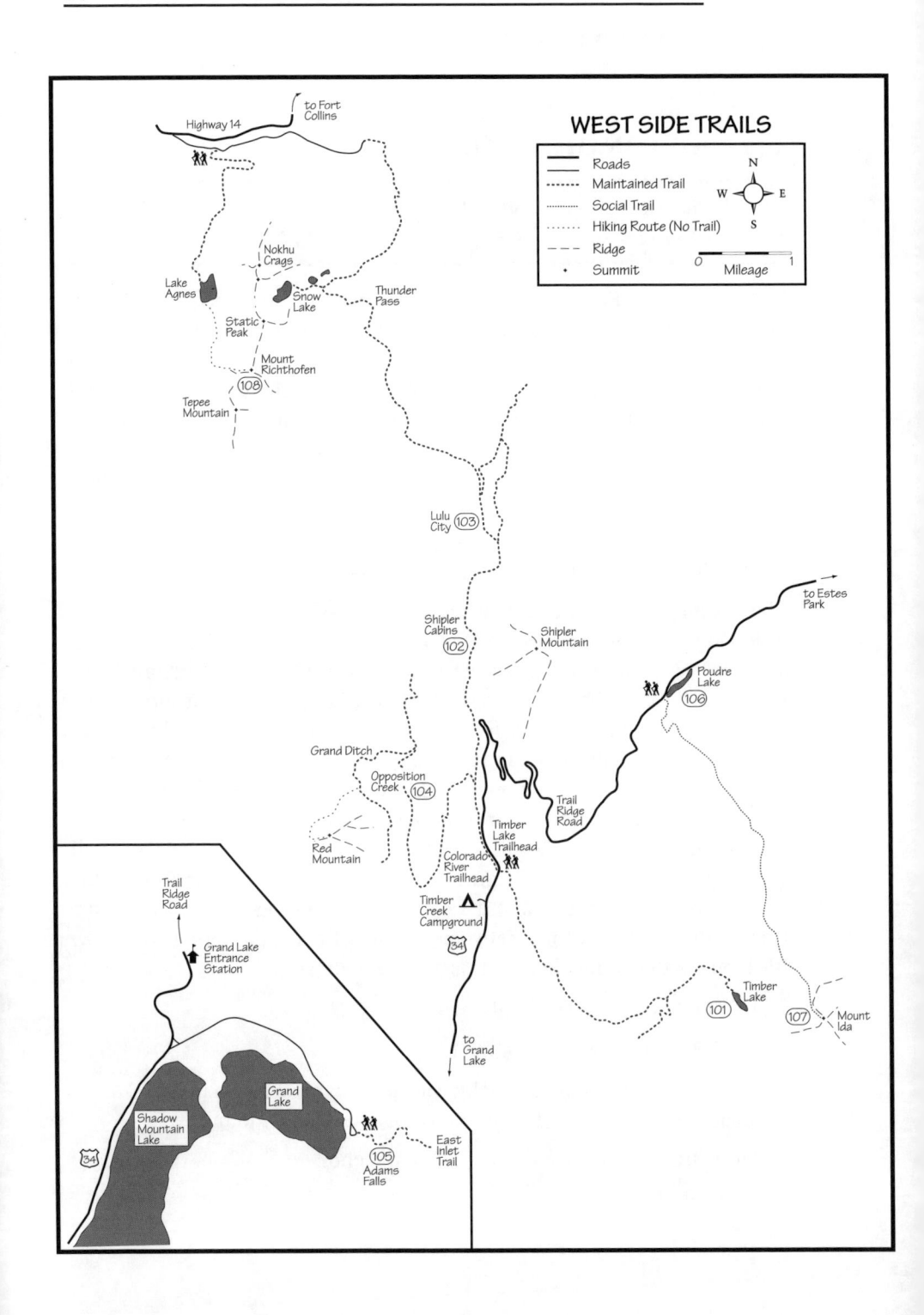

101 TIMBER LAKE

Distance	Altitude	Elevation Gain	Difficulty
5 miles	11,100 ft	2100 ft	moderate

Maps: 88, 90, 92. Now that you have seen the western slope (on the Tonahutu trail, No. 100), it is time to check out a few hikes on the far side of the Continental Divide.

LECTOR: What if I'm from Oregon? Then Estes Park is on the far side.

AUCTOR: Somehow I assumed that everybody starts from the east side. I live in Estes Park.

LECTOR: Congratulations. But you shouldn't assume.

From wherever you are, drive to the Timber Lake trailhead on Trail Ridge Road, some two miles north of Timber Creek Campground on the west side of the Park. Follow the trail south and east to the lake, which is not as scenic as the lakes at tree line tend to be on the east side, but is nonetheless a lovely place for lunch.

102 SHIPLER CABINS

Distance	Altitude	Elevation Gain	Difficulty
2.5 miles	9,100 ft	100 ft	easy

Maps: 90, 92. This hike starts at the Colorado River trailhead, directly across Trail Ridge Road from the Timber Lake trailhead (No. 101). Except for a short, sharp rise at the beginning, the trail follows a gentle gradient up the Colorado River (mostly north), sometimes within a few feet of the water. About half a mile from the parking lot, a trail branches left, heading for Red Mountain. It is worthwhile to turn off on this trail for a few yards, just to cross the bridge over the river (which goes to the Gulf of California, carving out the Grand Canyon along the way).

Returning to the Colorado River trail, continue northward through lovely meadows, an impressive rockfall (from a steep hill on the right), and a stand of willows. Soon the ruins of the old Shipler cabins appear, followed immediately by a sign indicating a privy in the woods to the left. The path to the privy continues faintly beyond it, descending a few feet to a fine lunch spot next to the river (now running swiftly over sparkling rapids).

92   A HIKING GUIDE TO RMNP

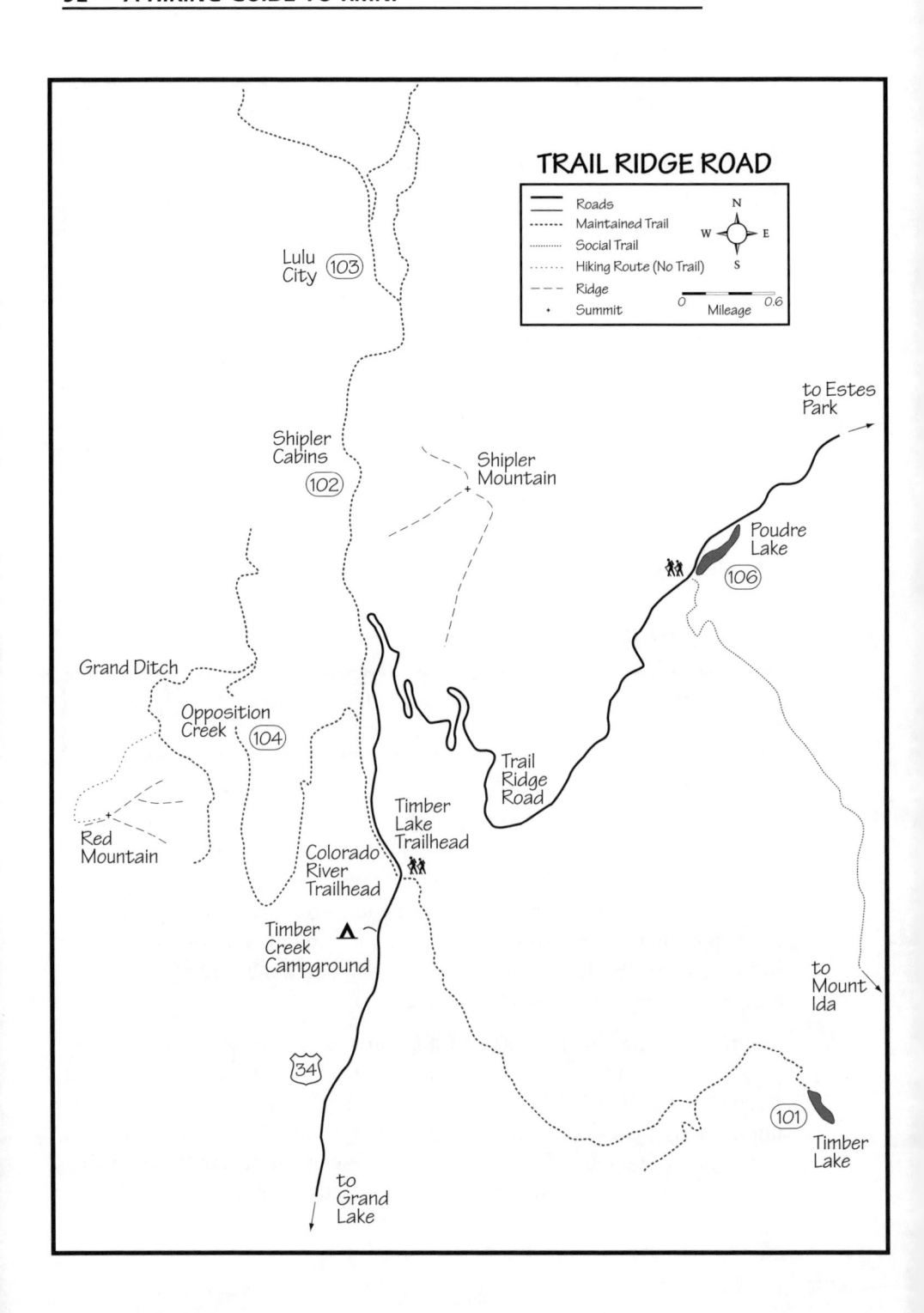

TRAIL RIDGE ROAD

- — Roads
- ····· Maintained Trail
- ······ Social Trail
- ······ Hiking Route (No Trail)
- – – Ridge
- • Summit

0 — 0.6 Mileage

Lulu City (103)

Shipler Cabins (102)

Shipler Mountain

Grand Ditch

Opposition Creek (104)

Red Mountain

Timber Lake Trailhead

Colorado River Trailhead

Trail Ridge Road

Poudre Lake (106)

to Estes Park

Timber Creek Campground

34

to Grand Lake

to Mount Ida

Timber Lake (101)

103 LULU CITY

Distance	Altitude	Elevation Gain	Difficulty
3.5 miles	9,400 ft	400 ft	moderate

Maps: 90, 92. Continue north from the Shipler Cabins (No. 102) for another mile to a fork in the trail. The right branch heads up to Poudre Pass, while the left branch goes downhill on a couple of switchbacks to Lulu City. There are several good lunch spots in the meadow, and along little streams flowing into the Colorado River, but hardly any evidence that miners were once active here. Thus does the wilderness reclaim what its citizens abandon.

104 OPPOSITION CREEK

Distance	Altitude	Elevation Gain	Difficulty
3 miles	9,900 ft	900 ft	moderate

Maps: 90, 92. Starting at the Colorado River trailhead (see No. 102), hike north for half a mile to the Red Mountain trail, which branches off left (west) to cross the Colorado River. Passing through a lovely meadow, it soon heads uphill to its first meeting with Opposition Creek. While this spot is already a good place for lunch, it is worthwhile to continue south on the mile-long stretch that eventually switches back north for another mile to cross Opposition Creek again.

It is not worthwhile to go much farther—unless you are interested in the Grand Ditch, a half-mile onward and upward. There is nothing grand about the ditch, nor about the service road that runs alongside it. To climb Red Mountain, you can hike west and south on the road for a mile or more, crossing Mosquito Creek and Opposition Creek yet again, until you decide it is time to scramble up the mountain. We advise against it. Have lunch back at the second crossing of Opposition Creek, and save your energy for better things.

105 ADAMS FALLS

Distance	Altitude	Elevation Gain	Difficulty
0.5 miles	8,500 ft	100 ft	easy

Maps: 88, 90. Take US 34 to the town of Grand Lake, and drive around the north side of the lake to the West Portal of the Adams Tunnel (which runs under the Continental Divide to supply water to the other side of the mountains). The East Inlet trailhead is a short distance farther, at the end of an unpaved road. Adams Falls is less than half a mile up the trail, a spectacular spot that is heavily visited. You can hike on up the trail toward the chain of lakes below Boulder-Grand Pass on the Continental Divide (see No. 93, page 84), but even the first lake is a long way off. Have lunch at the falls.

106 POUDRE LAKE

Distance	Altitude	Elevation Gain	Difficulty
0	10,800 ft	0	none

Maps: 90, 92. This is right off the road at Milner Pass on Trail Ridge Road, where a sign informs the traveler that the waters divide here. Take a picture of the sign and have lunch.

107 MOUNT IDA

Distance	Altitude	Elevation Gain	Difficulty
4.5 miles	12,880 ft	2,100 ft	moderate

Map: 90. You can climb Mt. Ida from Timber Lake (No. 101, page 91), but it is easier to start at Milner Pass (see No. 106). The trail goes up from the south end of Poudre Lake, and then follows the Continental Divide to the summit. The view is fine in all directions, but especially so down into Forest Canyon, where the Gorge Lakes nestle on various levels. It is tempting to climb down to some of these lakes (from a low point on the ridge between Mt. Ida and Mt. Julian), but the temptation is best resisted.

LECTOR: Oscar Wilde said the best way to overcome temptation is to give in to it.

AUCTOR: He is not the best person to imitate.

LECTOR: Don't you like *The Happy Prince?*

AUCTOR: "Bring me the two most precious things in the city," said God to one of His Angels; and the Angel brought Him the leaden heart and the dead bird.

LECTOR: "You have rightly chosen," said God, "for in my garden of Paradise this little bird shall sing for evermore, and in my city of gold the Happy Prince shall praise me."

AUCTOR: We seem to have found something in common. But I like the story better than its author.

WEST SIDE TRAILS 95

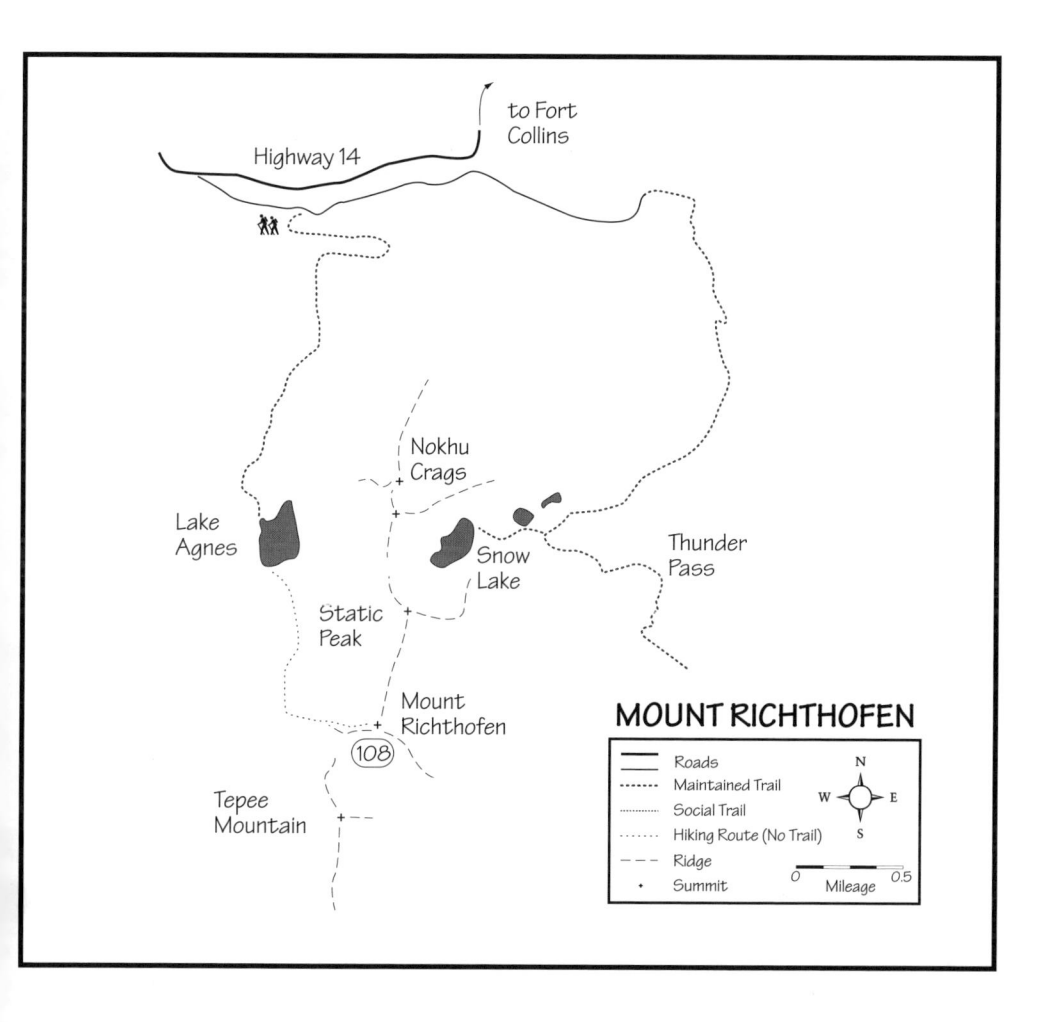

108 MOUNT RICHTHOFEN

Distance	Altitude	Elevation Gain	Difficulty
2 miles	12,940 ft	2,600 ft	hard

Maps: 90, 95. Drive up Colorado 14 from Ft Collins, over Cameron Pass to the Agnes Lake turn-off about three miles beyond the pass. Follow this road to the trailhead, then hike past Lake Agnes and climb south to the low point of the ridge between Richthofen and Mt. Mahler (to the west). Turn left (east) and work up the ridge to the top. It is a strenuous climb, but well worth the effort. Lunch at the top is inspiring.

109 THE GREEN DRAGON

Distance	Altitude	Elevation Gain	Difficulty
0	7,500 ft	0	none

This is fictitious. It represents the many fine eating places in Estes Park, at one of which you should have your last lunch (figuratively). Tell the proprietor we sent you, and put the book on the table, title side up. This will lead to questions, which you may answer as you choose, but we recommend some reference to the lunch spots preceding this one.

    LECTOR: Are you suggesting we should help you sell books?

    AUCTOR: When I am dead, I hope it may be said: "His sins were scarlet, but his books were read."

    LECTOR: You're still stealing from Hilaire Belloc.

    AUCTOR: He is beyond caring.